Sweet Magic

ALSO BY MICHEL RICHARD

Happy in the Kitchen
Home Cooking with a French Accent

Sweet Magic

EASY RECIPES *for* DELECTABLE DESSERTS

Michel Richard

with Peter Kaminsky

Illustrations by Michel Richard

ecco

An Imprint of HarperCollinsPublishers

HarperCollins books may be purchased for educational, business, or sales promotional use. For information, please write: Special Markets Department, HarperCollins Publishers, 10 East 53rd Street, New York, NY 10022.

FIRST EDITION

Designed by Mary Austin Speaker

Library of Congress Cataloging-in-Publication Data has been applied for.

ISBN: 978-0-06-192821-5

10 11 12 13 14   MT-PPB   10 9 8 7 6 5 4 3 2

To Gaston Lenôtre

Contents

Smiles and Delights

I recall a memorable and satisfying meal that was
served to a small group at the chef's table in Michel
Richard's restaurant Citronelle in Washington, DC.
We sat down that night at ten thirty—me, Michel, and
a gathering of chefs. Thomas Keller had just finished
an event in Michel's private dining room, where he
had presented dishes from his new cookbook to a
worshipful crowd. The hush that came over the

diners assembled for Thomas's event was akin to the collective holding of breath that comes over baseball aficionados when it is the last pitch of a possible no-hitter. Just down the street, at the Four Seasons Hotel, the ever-ebullient Jacques Pépin had finished a book signing for his latest work. Now it was time to eat. Michel had invited them and a few other close friends (also chefs) for supernal *côte de boeuf*—sliced off the bone—potatoes fried in clarified butter, *no* green vegetables, Epoisses cheese of such pungency that it conjured memories of a trash bin outside a fish market on a hot day. For dessert, Michel set out a bowl of what looked like chocolate-covered almonds: perfect ovals covered in chocolate and dusted with cocoa powder.

I reached for one, bit into it. But instead of the crunch of almond, I encountered the soft flesh of . . . I couldn't quite place it for an instant and then my brain sorted out the signals from Michel's surprise attack on my palate: It was a juicy seedless grape.

Typical Michel, I thought, presenting one thing disguised as another, using dessert as an opportunity to create a *trompe bouche*, so to speak. As they bit into the chocolate grapes, the assembled chefs expressed their delight with the burbling chuckle that is the only practical way to laugh with full mouth. This recipe would later appear in our book *Happy in the Kitchen*, but the larger point, that dessert should delight and bring forth a smile, is the guiding principle of this book too.

Another observation from that night: The only thing "gourmet" about the meal with the top chefs was the perfection of the ingredients and the precision of their preparation. Other than that, the dishes were simple, and the presentation was the opposite of "cheffy," by which I mean the components weren't piled up in Frank Gehry–like constructions, nor were they adorned with teeny tiny chopped vegetables and plated with artsy brushstrokes of something that had started out as a magnum of expensive wine reduced to three or four molecules.

No foams. No weird frozen nitrogen concoctions. Just great food.

That is the idea behind this book: to share the creative impulses of one of the greatest dessert masters in the world in a way that is simple, light (or at least lighter than traditional recipes), and as quick as technology and practical shortcuts will allow.

In the course of preparing these fifty desserts, you will make all the basic doughs of the modern pastry chef, but often in a lighter, less labor-intensive way. I can promise that you will never taste a flakier pie crust. You will discover—if you haven't discovered already—that where tradition calls for double boilers and thermometers, the microwave oven often saves time and cuts down on cleanup while sacrificing nothing in the way of results. You will work with chocolate, fruits, and gelatin. You will learn how to use the most basic meringue to lighten up pastry creams and mousses so that even "heavy" desserts are light.

These desserts can be fussed over and sculptured to justify a high price tag in an expensive restaurant, but all of them are really designed to be baked (or whipped or chilled) and brought to the table without a lot of bother. It's the texture and taste that matter. That's what always comes first with Michel Richard.

I know he put his heart and soul into these recipes, because every time he tried something new, at every step of the process, he would lick his fingers clean. If he went back for a second lick—the verdict was a happy one. If he paused after one lick—the underachieving dessert was tossed into the trash and, after considering things for a minute, Michel would start all over again.

Everything in this book got two licks.

—Peter Kaminsky

The Making of a Chef

You know the old expression: "If you can't stand the heat, get out of the kitchen." For me, the kitchen in question felt like I was stepping into an air-conditioned movie theater on the hottest day of August. You see, my first job—at fourteen years of age—was working in a bronze foundry. Forget any complaints you may have heard about working around 500-degree ovens. I was working with 1,000-degree molten metal.

I hated my job. My mom could plainly see that when I dragged myself home after a long day at the inferno. My hands were dry. My skin was dry. I felt that I looked as wrinkled and leathery as an alligator. One evening my mother reminded me I had once told her that I thought I might like being a cook.

Neither of us knew much about how you went about becoming a cook, but Mom had a friend who had an opinion about everything. One of those opinions was that I would be a better cook if I learned how to bake first. As I think back on it, I wonder, even though my parents were separated at the time, could this have had anything to do with the fact that my father was a baker? Such psychology was beyond me. All I knew was I needed a job. A few more links in the Mom-and-her-friends network produced an offer in our little town of Carignan, which is why, on the morning of September 1, 1962, I put on a new white coat—I was so proud!—and began the first of nearly a thousand days in the shop of Monsieur Jacques Sauvage.

Being a chef, and in particular being a pastry chef, was not a glamorous profession at that time. But I was young and needed to learn a craft, even one that paid ten dollars a month.

In the beginning, Mr. Sauvage had me making deliveries as much as he had me learning pastry—sort of a French pastry shop's version of the way that kung fu masters would make their disciples carry water up the mountain for a year before they learned the first thing about combat. Like all grown men, as I look back on my boyhood now I find that some little adventures stand out in my memory.

To this day, when winter comes, I still think of the time in 1964 when Mr. Sauvage and I went to deliver cakes in the nearby village of Mouzon. The roads were slick with ice; sleet fell from the sky and covered the windshield. We arrived at the shop of one of our customers and parked across the street. I slipped and slid across the pavement, nearly killing myself. The only way I could make it to the door of the shop was to crawl on my hands and knees. That was all Mr. Sauvage needed to see. Rather than risk the hazardous ice-skating course himself, he moved the car farther up the road, parked directly above me, and, one by one, slid the cake boxes down the icy street. I caught them and handed them to the owner of the shop.

I spent three years with Sauvage—making pastry creams, puff pastry, éclairs—learning the most basic of basics and repeating each operation ten thousand times until I suspect I could have performed most of them in the dark.

After Monsieur Sauvage, I was ready for the next step up the chef's ladder, as I had passed my CAP exam (Certificat d'Aptitude Professionnelle). I could now call myself a pastry chef at the little shop that hired me in Charleville. As any of you who have visited France know, bread is baked in one kind of shop—a *boulangerie*—and pastry is made in another, a *pâtisserie*. But there wasn't really enough business in Charleville to be one or the other, so we were both. The work was hard, but my salary went up 700 percent, plus I had a free bed to sleep in over the shop.

Things seemed okay until, four or five months after I went to work in this shop, which out of charity shall remain nameless, I plopped into bed, bone tired after an eighteen-hour day. I was just drifting off to sleep when I felt something big and warm and fuzzy moving around my legs. Terrified, I leaped out of bed, pulled back the covers, and uncovered Monsieur le Rat, who must have been as scared as I was, because he shot across the floor, scampered up the drainpipe, and disappeared.

The very next morning, I followed my furry bunkmate off the premises and out into the world. In other words, I quit.

Now what?

Like many young men before me, I joined the army. Instead of sending me off to win glory for my nation on the field of battle—which would have been hard at the time, because we were at war with no one—the generals in charge of the safety of the Republic took one look at me and knew where I belonged. They made me a cook. I was detailed to Paris during the height of the student-led strikes of 1968 and ordered to pick up the garbage that striking sanitation workers had left to pile up in the streets.

It wasn't very glamorous work, but it did one good thing for me—in fact, a great thing—it got me to Paris. I fell in love with *Paree* and, shortly after leaving my military service, I began a string of jobs in what I had hoped would be one glorious pastry shop after another.

But my romantic notions of perfect pastry in sumptuous showcases as fashionable and charming as any creation of the masters of haute couture were not yet to be. Instead, I worked in plenty of average pâtisseries. I made thousands of "buttery" croissants—*hold the butter* (margarine was the preferred cost-cutter)—and carloads of "vanilla" pastry cream—*hold the vanilla* (harsh, often artificial extract was the norm). I worked hard, but I was a bit ashamed of my profession. When asked what I did for a living, I often told people I was an artist—an impression that was no doubt strengthened when it turned out that my paycheck couldn't even cover the rent. Just like a real starving artist!

And then, a marvelous, life-changing event occurred. My friend Gérard was also in the business and invited me to his birthday celebration. A group of half a dozen of us had gathered for the party when Gérard arrived with a pretty box that he opened to reveal an absolutely gorgeous cake. Actually, that doesn't do it justice. It was the *Absolutely Most Gorgeous Cake in the History of the Universe.*

Who had made such a cake? Who was this Caravaggio of Croissants, this Leonardo of Layer Cakes, this Gauguin of Ganache?

There was a name on the box . . . *Gaston Lenôtre*.

Have you ever noticed how your own name seems to leap out at you from a printed page? Well, that's how Gaston Lenôtre's grabbed my attention.

"Who is this genius?" I asked.

"He's my boss," Gérard replied.

"I *must* meet him," I said, and Gérard wrote down the address for me: 44 rue Auteuil.

The very next morning, I took the Metro to Auteuil and approached the pastry shop with a look on my face like that of a small boy in front of the prettiest, brightest, most sparkling Christmas tree ever imagined. *Truly*, I thought, *this is a jewelry store of dessert.*

I called Gérard. "Do you think it would be possible for someone like me to find a job there?"

"Sure," he said, "they're looking for new employees."

I summoned up all the courage I had and called Mr. Lenôtre's office.

"Oh, he will want to see you in person," his friendly assistant said. "But he is in New York this week."

I was even more in awe. I had placed a call to a pastry chef who was so important that he was in New York!

"He'll be glad to see you when he returns," the nice lady told me.

On the day before our appointment, I went to the barber and, afterward, bought myself a new tie. As I checked myself out in the mirror, I told my reflection, "You look like a nice young man. I would hire you."

My mood had changed, or at least my confidence had drained, by the time I got to 44 rue Auteuil. I looked at my reflection in the window of his shop and thought, *I can't go through with this.*

I turned on my heel and walked back to the Metro stop. There were two ladies ahead of me on the stairs, each carrying a bag from Lenôtre. They outdid each other in saying how delicious the desserts were.

I reversed course again and went up to Lenôtre's shop. Without giving myself time for any more second thoughts, I strode up to the person in charge and said I was there for an interview with Monsieur Lenôtre.

"Up one flight and knock on the door," I was told.

I knocked.

"*Mon grand*, come in," a voice said, using a French term that translates as an affectionate form of "big guy." It was a nickname that I would hear a thousand times during my years with Lenôtre—but I am getting ahead of myself.

I opened the door and entered. Lenôtre, who had the most piercing blue eyes, turned toward me. Seated beside him, a secretary, with his pencil poised, waited to record our meeting. I am not sure how long we talked. I was in a dream, exchanging pleasantries with the god of desserts. I have a strong memory of his describing desserts and techniques that I knew nothing about. I confessed my ignorance, sure that I was sealing my fate.

"Michel, *mon grand*, we have 315 chefs in our company (he had more than one facility). Nobody has to know *everything*. When can you start?"

"When do you want me?"

He gave me the most fabulous one-word answer: "Tomorrow."

And so began my years with Lenôtre. In one day I was transformed from someone who was thinking seriously about leaving the business into a lifelong disciple of the Master. Even though he is gone, I remain his student.

I still have a strong impression of my first look at his pastry makers at work on a gorgeous wedding cake; Lenôtre told me that when people order a cake for their wedding, they want it to be the most beautiful, special cake ever made. Of course, they can't all be the best, but the customer should still have that feeling at the moment the cake is presented. Truly, it seemed that no cake could be better than the one I saw that first morning, with its beautiful sugar work of flowers, leaves, and songbirds. I felt a sense of pride and the hope that one day I would be one of those grand chefs.

It was a different work environment from any I had known before. Every morning, Lenôtre shook the hand of every employee, all three hundred of us! "*Bonjour, mon grand,*" he said to start my day. I began to love mornings and looked forward to seeing dawn (we began at five A.M.). The day was still fresh, the streets were quiet, and even stray dogs and alley cats were all peacefully asleep. The world was writing a new page, one that always began with the word *hope*.

Before Lenôtre, I knew that pastry could be delicious and seductive, but I had no idea that it could reach the level of beauty and perfection that came out of his workrooms. I remember seeing a sugar piece done by Mr. Rousselet—the master of sugar work at Lenôtre. He had won the Championnat de France award. Everything about it was just perfect. Every station at Lenôtre's had a similar master of his craft, and I worked my way through them, concentrating on learning each aspect of my trade. But no matter where I was, I was drawn to the grand spectacle of Mr. Rousselet at work on his sugar pieces. When I was done with my shift at another station, I would stand nearby and watch him, admiring him all the while.

I would go home in the early afternoon, buy sugar at the minimart downstairs from my home, and labor for hours, trying to achieve something similar to Mr. Rousselet's. Sugar work is like glassblowing, only done with liquid sugar instead of liquid glass. Finally, after hundreds of sad-looking efforts, the flowers I had been working on started to look real. I was so proud of myself, but not as proud as the day I created my first bird out of sugar. I stayed up all night admiring it! I also practiced writing at home. I would buy cheap toothpaste and practice writing on any washable surface in my kitchen. I used toothpaste because it had the same texture as chocolate and I was able to scoop it up and reuse it over and over. At last, there came a day when we had a lot of orders, more than usual. Mr. Lenôtre asked me if I could help decorate, and I quickly agreed. I was a little nervous, but I soon calmed down and showed that I could do it. Everyone was amazed, including me! In my mind, after that day, I considered myself a real Lenôtre pastry chef.

Lenôtre wasn't interested in looking for shortcuts or pinching pennies. My days of dealing with cheap flour, margarine, and artificial flavors were gone. All that he cared about was making the best: using the best Charentes butter (made from 100 percent cream), the richest most flavorful chocolate from Venezuela, the best vanilla from the rain forests of Madagascar. In four years, I never heard him talk about labor or food costs. All we talked about was quality: How can we make it better?

At this stage of his career, Lenôtre wasn't doing that much hands-on chef work, but he was always thinking about new desserts, dreaming up new ideas, new techniques, asking about new equipment. He encouraged us to do the same. I didn't need much coaxing. It seemed to come naturally to me. But the world of Lenôtre, like any business organization, was full of politics. It wouldn't look good for a young upstart to be blabbering on about his new ideas all the time, especially if they were good ideas. That's the perfect way to create a lot of jealousy. You had to be discreet about it, but Monsieur Lenôtre would notice.

One day, in 1973, he asked me to come into his office.

"*Mon grand*," he said, "how would you like to go to New York?"

I thought he was asking if I would like to visit New York. That would have been very exciting, but that wasn't it. Mr. Lenôtre wanted to open a pâtisserie on Fifty-ninth Street in Manhattan, between Park and Lexington avenues. You couldn't have had a more chic address. You also couldn't have imagined a younger person in charge—Lenôtre wanted me to be the chef. Years later, he told me that he thought I was the best pastry chef he had ever had, but at the time, I have to confess I felt a little intimidated by "le Grand Apple."

It was a beautiful shop. I didn't know it at the time, but one of my regular customers was my coauthor, Peter Kaminsky, who worked around the corner at *National Lampoon*. He tells me that he and his colleagues often had "the munchies." I am discreet enough not to ask him why.

But, as many of the top names in French gastronomy found as they opened and closed restaurants in Manhattan, native New Yorkers may be willing to spend a fortune on food in France, but not in America. Our desserts were way too expensive and, I think, a bit too sophisticated. In France, when you are invited to someone's home for dinner, you often bring a great bottle of champagne and the prettiest pastry you can afford. This is not so much the custom in America. People are as likely to make desserts as they are to buy them. This was bad for Mr. Lenôtre's venture, but I think it may be a good thing for those of you making the recipes in this book: Americans, with all their pies and cookies and layer cakes, are by and large better dessert makers than your average French home baker.

Excuse me, Maman and all the French mothers who turned out so many of my favorites, but it is true. Pick up any church cookbook at a local bake sale in America, and the biggest section is usually pies and cakes and cookies.

A little more than a year after we opened, Lenôtre New York piped its last éclair. It was July 14, Bastille Day. I didn't feel like celebrating, but America had won the heart of this young chef. Like millions of hopeful young immigrants before me, I decided to make my way in this new and exciting land.

Next stop, Santa Fe, where I opened my own pastry shop and also offered some appetizers and main courses for takeout or for customers to enjoy in an area set aside for a café. Meanwhile, the biggest names in the French restaurant world tried to bring their haute cuisine (and haute prices) to America. Acting on Mr. Lenôtre's recommendation, they often came to me for advice, and every one of them invited me back to France to learn about the nondessert side of cuisine. It took me ten years, but finally I was ready to open my own restaurants, first in Los Angeles and finally in Washington, DC.

Through all these years, I have remained a dessert maker at heart. Even when I serve a steak or rack of lamb or poached cod, I try to approach every recipe with the same spirit of fun and surprise that comes naturally to the dessert chef. In this book I want to give you the same injection of love and playfulness that Mr. Lenôtre gave me, and the lesson that dessert is a gift for your guests. I believe that people like desserts the way they like puppies or small children. Dessert makes you smile. When you make a good dessert, you feel proud. You know every one of your guests or family members is going to be happy. This is a truth I have observed after serving a million desserts (at least, maybe ten million). The desserts in this book are not designed for the showcase or the pricey menu. Instead, I have tried to take all the tricks and all the deliciousness of the greatest desserts and to make them accessible and uncomplicated.

If you follow these recipes—and more important—understand them and invent your own, you will always be a winner. Remember, the goal is not perfection . . . it is pleasure.

Is Dessert Necessary?

Nobody's mother ever said, "If you don't finish your chocolate cake, there'll be no beets for you!" Dessert is the part of the meal that is completely voluntary. You don't need it in order to survive, but you do need it, or at least *I* need it, to be happy with a meal. I guess I would call dessert a necessary luxury or maybe a luxurious necessity.

What is it about dessert that makes this so?

Of course it has something to do with our childhood love of sweets. You never outgrow your sweet tooth, so dessert is the part of the meal where the child inside is invited to come out and play. I'll bet that even Genghis Khan was pleasant when his servants brought him walnuts and honey sprinkled with rosewater. Although his pastry chef probably put his life on the line if he ever served the boss a soggy pie crust.

Love of sweetness is in our everyday language. We talk about someone we like being a "sweet person." It's a way of saying that someone makes us feel good in just the same way that dessert is easy to like. Sweetness is the only taste that is used to describe a person positively. Calling someone salty, sour, or bitter is never taken as a compliment. Tell people that you think they are sweet, and you are liable to make them feel so good they will sometimes blush like a ripe strawberry. Tell the same people that you find them bitter, and watch their expression wrinkle up like a dried apricot.

Dessert is a chance to put the world aside and indulge in the joy of the moment. When I am with my friends and we are sitting around a table, taking pleasure in each other's company, dessert is a way to make the moment last. Usually it's the nicest of interludes. In my decades as a chef, I have seen plenty of tense and angry times at the table, but very rarely when dessert is served. It's as if dessert calls a truce in our conflicts so we can simply enjoy our food and our dinner companions.

The only argument I ever see around dessert is this: Who gets the last bite?

Sweet Magic

Dessert making and savory cooking are closely related crafts, but there is a very big difference—apart from the obvious one that the pastry maker is an artist who creates variations on one theme, sweetness, while the cook invents soups, appetizers, and entrées that combine flavors and emphasize each one.

The most significant difference is that the cook can taste things throughout the process and adjust the balance of flavors, the thickness of sauces, the crust on a piece of meat *while* he or she is cooking. The changes are immediate. On the other hand, the pastry maker has to combine the ingredients for a dough or crust, fill it with fruit or cream or chocolate—and then wait to see if the recipe works. The only thing one can do at that point is pray, or take a walk, or answer an e-mail. While the cook on the meat and fish station in a restaurant can add a little salt here or lemon juice there, the pastry chef has no choice but to patiently await the verdict of the oven.

Sometimes I feel as if I am in court, watching the door where the jury will come through and wondering what my fate will be. Did that lady peering with the pinched expression over her glasses dislike me? That heavy man who looked like he was enjoying a short nap—did I bore him? I feel that way about my ingredients: Will my cream curdle? Will my dough be cracklingly crisp, or dull and soggy? Will the ghost of my teacher and mentor, the great *pâtissier* Mr. Lenôtre, come back in a black robe with a black veil over his head and send me away from the kitchen?

Usually, in the case of a new dessert idea, the verdict is a hung jury—neither guilty nor innocent. Some things work, and some things need more work. Usually they need more work: a lighter meringue, a flakier crust, a less runny filling, etc.

I actually enjoy that part of my job. The very act of conceiving a new recipe—like the conception of a child—is, in itself, a pleasure and basic to human nature. Then when the bun comes out of the oven, so to speak, if it is not perfect, we have the pleasure of trying to make it newer and better next time. Oh, boy—reconception!

But first, there is always inspiration, an idea. My natural mode of thought is dreaming about tastes and ingredients and how to do new things with them. I encounter the world in terms of flavors, textures, aromas. Like a sponge, I soak in what I see going on all around. Right now I am watching my children have breakfast. Something simple: cornflakes and milk. I sit and stare. I concentrate. When I am in this state, my wife knows she will have to repeat whatever she might say to me because I am off somewhere, dreaming up a new dish. I am having an imaginary conversation with Mr. Lenôtre or my late great buddy Jean-Louis Palladin, or the sweet little girl named Nora who came to my restaurant last night and broke into a smile as bright as a campfire when she sank her spoon into a passion-fruit soufflé. I am always having conversations in my mind with my mentors, my colleagues, my friends, my customers.

"Go ahead, Michel," they say. "Listen to the ingredients."

I look at the cornflakes and the milk. What if I were to create very thin, very crisp pieces of potato and then, for milk, create a white soup using potato flour? Hmm . . . okay, some flavor of leeks in the soup too. The result would look like my children's breakfast cereal and milk but would taste like vichyssoise with extra crunch.

"Oh, you are a genius, Chef," my customers will say.

Genius? Hardly. Just watching my kids in the morning.

LIMITED INGREDIENTS, UNLIMITED IMAGINATION

When you hear the word *dessert*, it conjures up so
many colorful pictures, many more images than
main course or *appetizer*. Why is this so? The dessert
section of a menu is always the shortest. Likewise,
in any all-around cookbook, the nondessert recipes
far outnumber the cookies and cupcakes and pies and
puddings. Yet still, in the mind's eye, desserts sum-
mon up a greater variety of shapes and colors and
textures.

Part of the answer has to do with the inherent playfulness of dessert. It's a vacation from the act of merely providing fuel for your body. Consider this: If I say the word *vacation* to you, you might imagine yourself in a hundred fun places, from beachside to mountaintop to the Champs-Elysées. But if I look at your mental snapshot collection when I say the word *work*, you are not going to come up with such an interesting or fun variety of images as you imagine your office, store, car, or computer.

So dessert is playtime. It's off the clock, so to speak. We are psychologically predisposed to let the mind wander and play when we think of it.

Coming at the end of the meal, it must be assertive and bold, just like the fireworks that go off at the end of Tchaikovsky's *1812 Overture*. You need to end with a bang. After all the food and wine of a great meal, dessert has to make your palate wake up and take notice. The nice thing is, it usually does. Very few dessert plates come back to my kitchen with more than a sprinkling of crumbs on them. Somehow people can always find room for dessert . . . *all of it*.

But that is only part of the story. In terms of color, texture, and shape, there is, in fact, more variety in the dessert part of the menu than among the savory courses. I think this is true because the chef is forced to be creative with dessert in a way that steak or linguine or soup doesn't require. You see, we dessert chefs have a much more limited alphabet with which to write our literature.

When you get right down to it, almost all desserts contain some combination of butter, sugar, flour, water, cream, eggs, and sometimes chocolate. While it is true that these are versatile ingredients that can be beaten, melted, toasted, crystallized, mixed, whipped, baked, and chilled to form seemingly endless combinations, the dessert chef doesn't have the luxury of all the spices, herbs, fruits, vegetables, fish, meat, and poultry that the savory chef has. So the dessert maker must make the most of the one advantage he or she does have—the spirit of amusement and joy: playing with shapes, textures, temperature, and flavor.

Because the dessert alphabet is so limited, it is important to have the very best ingredients. I know from hard experience that this is the case. When I started as an apprentice, times were still hard in the aftermath of war and recovery. France was just getting poised to take off into the prosperity that marked the last quarter of the twentieth century. We had only white sugar and one kind of flour (pretty high gluten from Manitoba, Canada). And because it was so costly, butter was often replaced with margarine.

I can confess to you now that we used margarine, even though my chef told his clients it was butter. If that goo was butter, then my neighbor's cat is Placido Domingo. It was this horrid thing called Astra. It came in different-colored packages indicating different degrees of hardness. Green was for puff pastry, blue for buttercream . . . and so on.

I asked my boss why we said our pastry was made with butter if there was no butter in it.

"You are a stupid young man," he said. "Nobody uses butter in our profession. Margarine is cheaper!" he shouted, as if raising his voice made the margarine better.

It didn't, of course, but a few years later when I ended up in the shop with Lenôtre, we used only first-class ingredients. You could almost taste the difference in the very air. But even with the best of ingredients, your technique, attention to detail, and the ability to imagine flavors, aromas, and textures are essential to good desserts.

"It is difficult to make something good out of second-class materials," a wonderful Hungarian restaurateur in old Budapest once said, "but it is quite easy to spoil the first-class ones."

Bottom line: The dessert chef's main ingredients are limited, so always use the very best you can find. It's always worth it, and look at it this way: It's cheaper than buying it at the bakery.

MY SWEETNESS MUSE

Once upon a time, if you were a pastry chef, sweetness meant only one thing: sugar. It could be powdered or granulated, but it was always the same white and refined cane sugar. It had two functions. The first and most important one was to add sweetness. The second was to provide lightness and structure in whipped things such as meringues. Sugar also acts as a preservative (think of the shelf life of strawberry jam), but if your dessert isn't devoured within a day or so, I would worry less about shelf life and more about what you could have done better.

Over the years, I have come to see sugar more as a seasoning, a tool to highlight other flavors and nuances in a recipe. When it is looked at in this way, you will find that you can cut down on the sugar in many desserts without sacrificing the satisfaction that comes from offering a sweet to complete a meal.

This is a far cry from the pastry making that I learned in France. Back then, if we made a simple pastry cream—say one liter (a little bit more than a quart)—it called for twelve egg yolks and a pound of sugar! The sweetness was overpowering. Like many modern chefs, I have tried to lighten my desserts, cutting down on eggs, butter, and sugar (for example, see the pastry cream for the Cinnabun, page 85). These are still the Holy Trinity of dessert making, but in excess they lose a lot of their holiness. Too much sugar rests like a protective layer on your palate, making it incapable of picking up the wonderful little taste notes that mark a dessert as special. Generally my rule is that if you taste sugar first, then you have oversweetened your recipe. When you make a raspberry tart, the first flavor that should hit you is raspberry, not sugar.

Since everyone's palate is different, I recommend that as you make these recipes, you experiment with the amount of sugar you use. It should be just over the tipping point where you begin to taste sweetness. Sweetness is an ornament and, when properly used, a jewel. But you wouldn't want to wear a dress or suit made out of diamonds and, in the same way, you don't want a dessert that seems to be all sugar.

White sugar is useful because it is uniform, dependable, unvarying. It also absorbs moisture. When baked, it contributes to structure. These are all good things, but they are not the whole story of sweetness.

Brown sugar—which is white sugar mixed with molasses—adds depth and strength of flavor. It has a slightly licoricey and caramel flavor. It goes well with the butteriness of nuts (and the nuttiness of butter). Licorice and anise have a particular affinity for sweetness that helps tie together the elements of flavor in any recipe (in savory cooking, I find that tarragon, basil, and fennel, all of which have an aniselike accent, help showcase the sweetness in a soup, appetizer, or main course).

Caramel, which is nothing more than cooked white sugar, works like brown sugar or straight molasses in that it also adds some brawn-iness—I almost want to say meatiness—to the flavor of cane sugar. Depending on how long you cook it, caramel varies in delicacy and color. Mr. Lenôtre always liked to add a little caramel to his meringues to give them an attractive tan hue. I sometimes like to make caramel, let it harden, and then pulverize it. It's granular like white sugar, but toasted and deeper in flavor.

Molasses, which is a reduction of the juice of sugarcane left over in the processing of white sugar, lends moistness, color, and a smoky, earthy flavor to recipes (such as the Macadamia Chocolate Chip Cook-ies, page 140). In America there is a type of molasses made from sorghum. I was totally unfamiliar with this until Peter Kaminsky brought me a jar that he picked up from Newsom's Old Mill Store in western Kentucky (I knew its famous country hams but never this strange molasses). I tried substituting it for molasses in my pecan pie (page 172). I like it. I am going to find more ways to use this new (to me) ingredient. You should do the same, using it instead of honey or conventional molasses.

Honey is like a piccolo playing with a string quartet: you can't avoid noticing it. Honey can add a floral and, sometimes, a lemony element to the taste of a dessert. I am particularly fond of chestnut honey, which has a round and smooth taste. I am not so wild for other honeys. I can always pick out extraneous flavors that stand out from the harmony I am looking for in dessert. I don't use honey a lot, but when I do, I find it adds not only sweetness but moistness.

Don't let me forget to mention the sugar in fruit itself. Fruit sugars are distinct and varied. And when we peel an apple or pear, or discard its core, we are throwing out some natural sugar that the hardworking fruit tree has put into her little babies. I often make stocks out of the trimmings and bones of meat, fish, and poultry. For the same reason, I like to make fruit stocks, simmering and reducing the flavorful parts that don't get included in dessert. You also get an extra dose of thickener from the pectin in fruits such as apples, figs, and plums, which means you can thicken desserts with a fruit-flavored thickener rather than neutral-tasting cornstarch. See Soaked (but Not Soggy) Sponge Cake (page 53) for an example.

And let us not forget the wonderful sap of the maple tree, which gives us maple syrup and maple sugar. Nutty, sweet, deeply layered, it steps into recipes like a fine actor who knows how to play any role and make an impression without taking over the whole production.

Note: When using fluid sweeteners such as honey, maple syrup, or molasses, you will need less liquid in doughs and batters. I have adjusted the recipes in this book accordingly. You should be prepared to experiment when making your own substitutions.

THE INVISIBLE INGREDIENT

Bill Cosby has been a regular customer of mine for a
long time. Whenever he comes into the restaurant,
you can count on him to give the dining room and the
kitchen an impromptu performance that is different
every time. Years ago, he put out a comedy album
called *Why Is There Air?* It's the kind of question a
child would ask. But it is also one that is implied in
almost everything you bake or whip. While it's true
that pastry making depends on just a few fundamental

building blocks—eggs, butter, flour, water, cream, and sometimes chocolate—this overlooks one crucial ingredient. You cannot see it, feel it, hear it, smell it, or taste it. What is this strange thing that is so important but calls so little attention to itself? It is the very breath of life: *air*.

When we beat egg whites to form a fluffy meringue, all we are doing is creating bubbles—little packages filled with air—and adding some sugar to sweeten and stabilize the white cloud in the mixing bowl. If we heat the meringue, the sugar and egg proteins form a microstructure around these bubbles.

In a simple sponge cake (also known as genoise), whole eggs are aerated to make a foam. Then, in the process of baking, as the moisture in the mixture turns into steam, it fills these tiny air spaces and expands. Meanwhile, the proteins in the flour and the eggs unravel and delicately stretch and harden into airy structures that give the cake volume and its typically crumbly texture.

When we encase layers of butter between layers of flour and water in puff pastry, we are setting the stage for heat to melt the butter and steam to seep into the flour mixture, creating layers of air that expose the hundreds of pastry surfaces to heat. The layers then toast and acquire the most delicate crispness. The air between each two of the layers surrounds the flour mixture in the way that the air in an oven dries, toasts, and crisps the outside of a cake or bread.

Pie dough does the same thing, although not with neatly aligned layers as in puff pastry. Here, the little spaces that are filled with cold butter melt and the moisture released creates thousands of tiny air chambers that once again crisp and toast the flour mixture. In éclairs, the butter is more thoroughly combined with eggs and flour, and the result is that the moisture in the eggs and butter expands and then the flour and egg proteins encase the resulting trapped puffs of air.

Apart from lightness, the air that is captured in foams, batters, doughs, and mousses makes flavors more powerful and fuller. At first glance, you might think the reverse would be true: that more air would dilute and lessen the flavor. In fact, what I believe happens is that when ingredients stretch to form the surface of a bubble (or when they form lattices that maintain volume filled with air), you have much more surface area for each flavor component to roll over your tongue. I think this property has much to do with the current fad for foams in savory cooking. Without adding butter or other fat to a sauce, filling it with air lets each molecule of flavor come into contact with your tongue while releasing aromas that fill your palate and nose with taste and aroma.

So don't take air for granted. In fact I think the mark of a good chef is that he or she always thinks, "What happens deep down inside the cooking process when ingredients are touched by air?"

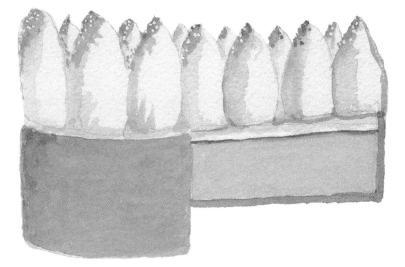

MY FAVORITE TOY

If I had to pick one technological advance that has revolutionized the chef's craft, it would surely be the microwave oven. Some chefs (usually at pricey, fine-dining restaurants) might choose the *sous vide* method that involves vacuum sealing ingredients in Cryovac plastic and cooking for a long time at very low temperatures. But the equipment is expensive.

Even without *sous vide*, what self-respecting gourmet could have missed the unmistakable trend toward treating recipes as chemical formulas? Molecular Gastronomy has been in the forefront of this movement, with chefs using liquid nitrogen and various other rarefied nonfood ingredients in an attempt to alter the basic nature of food (changing color, texture, and flavor). I am reminded of those eighteenth-century *grandes dames* in the court of Louis XV, whose elaborate coiffures looked like a storm-tossed ocean with a sailing ship riding atop the waves. One has to give credit for all the work that went into it, but truthfully, did it make Madame de Pompadour any more fetching than Audrey Hepburn in a ponytail?

The microwave is often overlooked when we tally up the ways in which technology has enriched and simplified the cooking process. Why? I think some of this has to do with a vein of snobbery that runs through the food world. The reasoning is "well, if midwestern housewives use it to reheat a bowl of chili, then what great chef wants to use a tool whose greatest utility seems to be to heat up leftovers?"

The short answer is, I do—and not just for leftovers. I have found that so much of the time-consuming, pot-dirtying work in cooking can be done away with simply by using the microwave oven.

I have basically stopped using a double boiler (*bain-marie* in French) for pastry creams and buttercreams (see A Happy Birthday Cake, page 189), for the tempering of chocolate (Chocolate Cups, page 29), for cooking puddings and custards (such as the maple pudding on page 157), for pie fillings (Quick Pecan Pie with Sorghum Molasses and Cranberry Curry Cream, page 172), for melting gelatin, or for softening butter (Choco-Mocha Layer Cake, page 58).

There are pastry purists out there who scoff when I tell them about my many microwave shortcuts, but far fewer once they try these out for themselves.

Fewer pots to clean, cooking in less time, and perfect results: I cannot imagine Escoffier disapproving.

PART I

My Sweet Dreams

The Ultimate French Toast

Dessert is not the only meal of the day for sweet things. Breakfast, for many people, is unthinkable without something sweet, whether it is a cinnamon bun, sugar in coffee, or waffles with maple syrup. From a cook's point of view, one of the nice things about breakfast foods is that they don't demand elaborate presentation. In making a dessert version of one breakfast favorite, French toast, my goal was to accent the sweet, warm, creamy, and comforting feeling of breakfast but to serve it as the final course at lunch or dinner. Few recipes can be guaranteed to please everyone. This one can.

✳ SERVES 9

CUSTARD AND TOASTS

½ cup whole milk

2 cups heavy cream

½ cup granulated sugar

1 teaspoon unflavored gelatin

2 vanilla beans, slit lengthwise,
    or 2 teaspoons vanilla extract

9 egg yolks, blended with a fork

18 slices firm white bread

BATTER

1½ cups whole milk

4 eggs

½ cup packed brown sugar

1 teaspoon cinnamon

½ teaspoon salt

Unsalted butter for frying

6 tablespoons turbinado sugar
    for finishing

Maple syrup for serving

Preheat the oven to 300 degrees.

To prepare the flan, whisk the milk, cream, granulated sugar, and gelatin in a heavy medium saucepan. Scrape the seeds from the vanilla beans into the pan and add the pods (or add the vanilla extract). Bring the mixture to a boil over medium-high heat, then remove it from the heat and let the beans steep for at least 1 hour, or until the mixture cools to room temperature. Discard the pods or wash and dry them and then add to a jar of granulated sugar to make a wonderfully scented sweetener.

Place a 9-inch square baking dish in a larger baking pan. Pour enough water into the large pan to come halfway up the sides of the baking dish. Remove the baking dish, carefully place the water-filled baking pan in the oven, and heat it for about 15 minutes.

Whisk the blended egg yolks into the cooled custard mixture and pour into the baking dish. Place the baking dish carefully into the warm water bath and bake until the custard is set and a knife inserted into the center comes out clean, about 45 minutes. Cool, cover, and refrigerate the flan until just before assembling the French toast. (The flan can be prepared up to 2 days in advance.)

To make the French toast, place 9 slices of the bread on a clean work surface. Remove the flan from the refrigerator and cut it into nine 3-inch squares, trimming them as necessary to make them even. Center a flan square on top of each piece of bread. Cover each flan with one of the remaining slices of bread. Cut off the crusts from the edges of the stacked bread slices to produce 9 square "sandwiches" and set aside.

Prepare the batter in a medium bowl by whisking together the milk, eggs, brown sugar, cinnamon, and salt. Dip each sandwich in the batter, coating both sides, and place it on a sheet pan lined with parchment paper.

Heat 1 tablespoon of the butter in a large nonstick skillet and place 2 or 3 of the sandwiches into the pan (as many as will easily fit). Using a metal spatula to flip the French toast as needed, cook for 1 to 2 minutes on each side, or until golden brown. Set aside on a clean baking sheet. Wipe out the skillet, add another tablespoon butter to the pan, and cook more sandwiches as above.

When all the French toast is cooked, preheat the broiler. Sprinkle the top of each French toast with 1 teaspoon turbinado sugar and place the sheet pan under the broiler for about 2 minutes, until the sugar is melted. Turn the sandwiches over, sprinkle them with turbinado sugar on the other side, and broil them for an additional 2 minutes.

Drizzle with maple syrup.

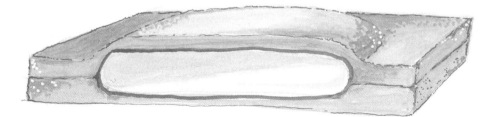

Coffee Crème Brûlée

You rarely see crème brûlée outside a restaurant or café. This puzzles me somewhat because it is a very simple recipe. I think making a crackling brûlée crust with a blowtorch is what scares people. Yes, there are petite blowtorches that are quite easy to use, but many home chefs are put off by the idea of a recipe that calls for the use of welding equipment. To remove this source of anxiety, I came up with the idea of making a crust out of a powder of caramel and chocolate. The result has the look of a perfectly crusted crème brûlée, with no blowtorch needed. The almost-burnt taste of caramel and the roasted cacao beans (from which the chocolate is made) match up perfectly with the roasted flavor of coffee in the sweet, vanilla-accented custard. ✳ SERVES 4

BRÛLÉE POWDER
1 cup packed brown sugar
2 tablespoons water
8 ounces roughly chopped
   semisweet chocolate, frozen

COFFEE CUSTARD
2½ cups whole milk
½ cup packed brown sugar, dark
2 teaspoons instant espresso powder
2 vanilla beans, split lengthwise, or
   2 teaspoons vanilla extract
2 teaspoons unflavored gelatin
4 egg yolks, blended with a fork

Start by making the brûlée powder. Combine the sugar and water in a small saucepan. Don't stir. Boil, still without stirring, until golden brown and caramelized, about 5 minutes. You can test the color of the sugar by spooning a bit of the syrup onto a white plate. The sugar is ready when it is golden brown. Pour the hot sugar onto a Silpat-lined sheet pan and cool completely.

Remove the chocolate from the freezer and chop it in a food processor until it looks like fine sand. Transfer to a bowl. Break up the caramelized sugar and pulverize it in the food processor until it is the size of small gravel. Add the sugar to the chocolate and stir to combine. Transfer to an airtight container and store in a dry, cool place until ready to use.

To make the custard, place the milk, sugar, and instant espresso in a large, heavy saucepan. Whisk the ingredients with a wire whisk until well mixed. Scrape the seeds from the vanilla beans* into the milk mixture (or add the vanilla extract). Place the pods in the saucepan and bring to a boil over medium-high, then remove the pan from the heat.

If you are using vanilla beans, let the beans steep in the milk mixture for 15 minutes. Discard the bean pods, or wash and dry them and then add to a jar of granulated sugar to make a wonderfully scented sweetener.

In a medium bowl, whisk ½ cup of the hot milk mixture and the gelatin into the egg yolks to gently warm the yolks so they don't curdle or cook. Then add them to the saucepan with the warm milk and whisk well. Pour the custard into individual

---

*   To avoid getting lumps of vanilla bean seeds when adding them to a liquid, try this process: Place 1 tablespoon of the sugar directly on a work surface. Scrape the beans on top of the sugar. Using the flat side of a knife, work the vanilla into the sugar. The natural oils from the vanilla bean seeds will be absorbed by the sugar and will separate the little granules more effectively.

1-cup crème brûlée dishes. Refrigerate for 2 hours to allow the custard to set.

Preheat the oven to 350 degrees. Sprinkle approximately 3 tablespoons chocolate brûlée powder over the top of each dish. Set the dishes in the oven for 10 seconds to slightly melt the chocolate. Refrigerate until serving time.

Chocolate Cups: A Happy Accident

Tempering chocolate—gently melting and then cooling it again so that it resets in the shape that you want—can be a real hassle and time-consuming, and requires very precise temperature management. This method is more like "quick tempering," and the result is a bowl or cup made entirely of chocolate. It never fails to impress.

It was completely by accident that I came up with this trick. One day in 1978, I was working on new recipes in the crowded little kitchen of my pastry shop in Los Angeles. I had left a bowl of melted chocolate on the counter. Next to it was a bowl with ice cubes from another recipe I was developing. In my haste to clear my workspace, I dropped one of the ice cubes into the bowl of warm chocolate. Knowing that chocolate and water don't mix very well, I grabbed the ice cube very quickly.

To my surprise, in those few seconds, the chocolate had set around the ice cube. At the same time, the heat of the chocolate had made the surface of the ice slightly wet, so that when I removed the cube from the bowl a perfect rectangular box made of chocolate slid off the ice cube.

I was intrigued by the possibilities of creating containers out of chocolate, so I started to experiment. I filled a glass with water—one of those old-fashioned champagne cups that are short and wide (the legend is that the original was molded from an impression of Marie Antoinette's breast). I floated a cork in it before I put it in the freezer so that when I removed the molded ice from the glass, I would have a handle to lift it with after dipping it into the chocolate.

The result was a chocolate bowl as perfectly shaped as Mme. Antoinette's original. Since that time, I have made chocolate containers using many different bowls, cups, and glasses as molds. I fill these edible containers with mousses, berries, pastry creams, meringues—anything that is soft and cool.

Note: The chocolate cups will last for about a month in a cool, dry place.

✳ MAKES 8 TO 10 CUPS

20 ounces bittersweet chocolate,

    chopped

Fill an 8-ounce coffee mug—or any other small cup or bowl—with water and use a piece of plastic wrap to cover it. Puncture a hole in the plastic and insert a Popsicle stick or plastic spoon into the water. Freeze for at least 4 hours, or until solid.

Once the water in the mug is frozen, line a sheet pan with a kitchen towel and place the chocolate in a microwave-safe bowl. Microwave for 1 minute on high and stir. Continue microwaving at 30-second intervals, stirring in between, until the chocolate is melted.

Release the frozen ice-pop by placing a very warm towel around the mug. If the ice-pop has some moisture on it, wipe it with a dry towel and immediately submerge it into the chocolate about three-quarters of the way up. Lift the ice-pop out of the chocolate, letting the excess drip back into the bowl. Gently drag the bottom of the dipped ice-pop along the rim of the bowl to remove any remaining liquid chocolate. Unmold the chocolate cup onto the cookie sheet by pushing gently down on it and popping it off the ice. Repeat eight or nine more times. If the chocolate begins to set, reheat it in the microwave for a few seconds until melted again and stir before continuing.

Note: To make these chocolate cups a little fancier, you can decorate the rims with such items as poppy seeds, crystallized or colored sugar, or toasted coconut. Place about ¼ cup of whatever you choose in a small bowl large enough to dip the cups into. Heat an empty cookie sheet in the oven or use a blowtorch to heat a small section of a cookie sheet. Place the top of a cup on the hot surface for a couple of seconds, just to melt it slightly. Immediately dip it into the bowl to create a decorative edge. Reheat the cookie sheet as needed to decorate more cups.

Cocoa Puff Chocolate Mousse Cups

This little recipe is full of happy surprises. The mousse itself is different from what you will find in many cookbooks. I make it without egg yolks. It is lighter, and you don't have to fuss over the precise right moment to put in the egg yolk. (Normally you have to watch the yolks like a mother hen guarding her chicks. If you put them in when the chocolate is too hot, they will cook rather than blend. If the mixture is too cool, it will seize up and become almost unmixable.) You can substitute this for any chocolate mousse in this book.

Cocoa Puffs cereal, covered with melted chocolate and then dusted with cocoa powder, adds layers of chocolate and crunch to this fluffy, light mousse. Your gourmet friends may turn up their noses at using Cocoa Puffs, so don't tell them the secret of these delicious little crunch balls until they have tasted them.

Hint: When microwaving chocolate, your goal is not to make it molten hot, just melted and warm to the touch. Overheating will throw the chocolate "out of temper." Without going into the fine points of the organic chemistry of chocolate, losing one's temper is never a good idea . . . for people or for chocolate.

✳ SERVES 6

CHOCOLATE MOUSSE CUPS
5 ounces dark chocolate, chopped
1 cup heavy cream
4 egg whites
2 tablespoons granulated sugar
Chocolate Cups (page 29)

COCOA PUFF TOPPING
2 ounces semisweet chocolate,
  chopped

1½ cups Cocoa Puffs cereal, frozen
¼ cup cocoa powder
Powdered sugar for sprinkling

To make the mousse, place the chopped chocolate in a micro-wave-safe bowl. Microwave on high, at 30-second intervals, stirring in between, until melted.

In the bowl of a stand mixer fitted with the whisk attachment, whip the cream until soft peaks form, about 2 minutes. Do not overwhip. Transfer to a clean bowl. Wash and dry the mixer bowl and whisk.

Place the egg whites into the clean mixer bowl and, using the whisk attachment, beat on high for about 1 minute, until the whites are foamy. Add the sugar 1 tablespoon at a time until soft peaks form. Gently fold the whipped egg whites into the whipped cream using a rubber spatula. Add about one-third of the melted chocolate to the cream mixture and fold until it is well mixed. Add the remaining chocolate, gently incorporating it with the rubber spatula. (The mousse is now ready to be used in any way you wish.)

To prepare the mousse cups, fit a pastry bag with the largest tip you have and fill it with the chocolate mousse. Pipe each of the chocolate cups three quarters full and set them aside somewhere cool while you prepare the topping.

For the topping, place the chocolate in a microwave-safe bowl and microwave on high at 30-second intervals, stirring in between, until melted. If you have a pair of disposable rubber gloves, put them on now. This will keep your hands clean and keep any moisture—or fingerprints—off the chocolate. The next step needs to be done quickly and will be easier if you have someone to help.

Remove the Cocoa Puffs from the freezer and pour them into the melted chocolate, tossing them quickly with your hands to coat them. Since the puffs are frozen, they will coat very quickly. If possible, have someone else hold the bowl steady and sprinkle the cocoa powder onto the puffs as you separate them from one another. Continue sprinkling the cocoa powder until all the Cocoa Puffs are separated.

Pour topping into each mousse cup until the puffs reach the top of the cup. Add a sprinkle of powdered sugar on top for a contrast of color.

Flan with Automatic Crust

One of my greatest pleasures since I came to America has been shopping in ethnic markets, looking for inspiration from new ingredients. The variety is dazzling. Other countries may have a Chinese neighborhood or an Ethiopian neighborhood, but the United States seems to have everything. As a Frenchman, I am well acquainted with couscous. Because of France's long—and not always happy—association with Algeria, you could always find couscous, but it was the kind with little grains. Large-grained Israeli couscous (also known as pearl pasta) was completely new to me when I came to America. I'm pretty sure that I was the first gastronomic chef to use it. In this dessert, the little balls of pasta swell and soften in the flan as it cooks and then they rise to the surface and toast. With no further encouragement, the couscous makes a nice crunchy crust all by itself. It's a great example of letting simple ingredients do the work for you.   * SERVES 6 TO 8

4 tablespoons (½ stick) unsalted
    butter softened to room tempera-
    ture so it has a mayonnaise-like
    consistency
1 cup Israeli couscous (pearl pasta)
8 eggs
1 quart half-and-half
1 cup packed brown sugar, dark
1 pinch salt
2 vanilla beans cut lengthwise or
    2 teaspoons vanilla extract*
Strawberry Cassis Sauce (see above)
    for serving

*   See note, page 27.

STRAWBERRY CASSIS SAUCE

....

½ cup Beaujolais or other
    fruity red wine
3 tablespoons honey
2 tablespoons crème de
    cassis
1 pint strawberries, washed,
stemmed, and sliced in half

In a medium bowl, whisk together the wine and the honey. Stir in the crème de cassis. Add the berries and mix to combine. Cover and refrigerate for at least 30 minutes before serving.

Smear the inside of an 8-inch round cake pan with the butter so the pan is generously covered.

Pour the couscous into the pan and shake it in a circular motion to help the beads adhere to the bottom and sides. There will be an excess of pasta, which should be removed by gently tipping the pan over a bowl to allow the extras to fall out. Place the pan in the freezer for at least 30 minutes.

While the cake pan is chilling, preheat the oven to 325 degrees.

In a medium bowl, mix the eggs, half-and-half, sugar, salt, and vanilla beans with a whisk until smooth. Place the prepared cake pan on a sheet pan and slowly, gently pour the egg mixture into the pan. This will fill the pan to the very top. Carefully place it in the oven and bake for 1 hour until set and center is a little jiggly. During baking, the couscous will rise through the custard to the top.

Allow the flan to cool completely, then invert it onto a serving plate so that the couscous forms a crust on the bottom. Refrigerate until serving time. Serve with the strawberry sauce.

Floating Islands with Melted Chocolate Morsels

Floating islands are among my family's favorite home desserts. The recipe used to be very labor-intensive. You would make a meringue, then poach it, then cool it in the refrigerator. After all that work, the result too often seemed like a very tired mousse, with a lot of sugar to compensate (which rarely improved it). Here, I call for the use of xanthan gum. It is made from fermented cornstarch and is one of the most powerful thickening agents. It is very popular with avant-garde Spanish chefs and allows you to make a super-light and stable meringue with less sugar.

Another thing that bothered me about the old-style floating island was that it was usually decorated with spun sugar. This meant that you tasted the sweetest part of the dessert first. I prefer flavors that progress from less intense to more intense (you don't drink a heavy Côtes du Rhone before moving on to a crisp Chardonnay). Acting on that principle, I incorporated little bits of chocolate into the meringue, then microwaved the whole thing. That way you have this light, not-too-sweet meringue, with intense bits of melted chocolate inside.

Note: If xanthan gum is not on your grocery store shelf, look for it under the Bob's Red Mill label in natural food stores.   ✳ SERVES 6

6 ounces semisweet chocolate,
   chopped and frozen
4 egg whites
½ teaspoon xanthan gum
½ cup granulated sugar
Hot Buttered Rum Sauce (page 41)
   or Red Berry Coulis (page 53)

Place the frozen chocolate pieces in a food processor and whir it into small granules. Transfer the ground chocolate to a small, covered, airtight container and refrigerate.

Place the egg whites and xanthan gum in the bowl of a stand mixer. Using an immersion blender, blend until the xanthan gum is well mixed, 10 to 15 seconds. Place the bowl on the mixer fitted with whisk attachment and whip on high for about 1 minute, until the whites are foamy. Add the sugar 1 tablespoon at a time. Continue to whip on high speed for 10 minutes until very stiff. Fold in the reserved ground chocolate with a rubber spatula.

Cover two large microwave-safe dinner plates tightly with sheets of plastic wrap. Gently spoon 3 mounds—about 3 inches in diameter and about 2 inches apart—onto each plate. (This can be done well in advance and refrigerated until just before serving time.)

Ten minutes before serving, microwave each plate on high for 10 seconds. Spoon the sauce of your choice onto serving plates and use an offset spatula to transfer each floating island to rest in the center.

Serving suggestion: Serve with additional rum sauce or berry coulis drizzled on top.

Rum Espresso Mousse

This mousse is a very simple use of whipped gelatin over ice. When I was a young chef, I would have made this with lots of cream and sugar. Or, later, when I started my quest for lighter desserts, I would have whipped cream and egg whites. But while experimenting with gelatin one day, I whipped sugar, espresso, and gelatin over ice—no cream, no egg whites—and I ended up with what I called a "coffee cloud." Add a little cream, or even nonfat milk, and it has the mouthfeel of a rich mousse. I toss in some rum—which is distilled from sugarcane—as a way of adding sugar but not more sweetness to the coffee flavor.   ✳ SERVES 10

MOUSSE
1 tablespoon dark rum
⅓ cup cold water
2 teaspoons unflavored gelatin
¼ cup packed brown sugar
2 cups freshly brewed espresso or
    strong coffee

WHIPPED CREAM
½ cup heavy cream
1 teaspoon granulated sugar

To make the mousse, in a small bowl, stir together the rum and water and sprinkle the gelatin on top. Let sit until the water has soaked into the gelatin, about 1 minute. Fill a very large bowl halfway with ice cubes, water, and a handful of salt, and set another large bowl into the ice water. Combine the brown sugar, coffee, and melted gelatin mixture in the bowl and whisk together. Continue whisking until mixture starts getting frothy, light, and cool. Using an instant-read meat thermometer, test the temperature—when it reaches 70 degrees, transfer the mousse to the bowl of a stand mixer fitted with the whisk attachment.

Beat at medium speed for 2 minutes (it might be a little splashy, so start at a lower speed). As the mousse starts to firm up, increase the speed to high and continue to whip until soft peaks form, about 1 minute longer. When the mixture is frothy and light and resembles foam, spoon it into glasses or coffee cups and chill it for at least 15 minutes. The longer you wait, the firmer it will get.

Just before serving, whip the cream in the chilled bowl of a stand mixer fitted with the whisk attachment, adding the sugar little by little until it holds soft peaks. Spoon whipped cream over the mousse.

Mulled Cider and Rum Risotto

I rarely eat rice except when it is cooked like risotto. Why? Because only then does it develop a smooth, creamy mouthfeel. This got me thinking: If I like that way of cooking rice in savory dishes, then why not in a dessert? As with my Ultimate French Toast (page 23), I took risotto, which is something that you don't normally eat as a dessert, and made it into one. If you want to go overboard and really pile up the tastes, serve this with Hot Buttered Rum Sauce (opposite). Serving suggestion: Ice cream and Cinnamon Crème Anglaise (page 163) are also suitable toppings.

* SERVES 4

RISOTTO

8 tablespoons (1 stick) unsalted
  butter
2 small Fuji apples, peeled, cored,
  and cut into ¼-inch dice
2½ tablespoons granulated sugar
1 tablespoon rum
1½ tablespoons vanilla extract
5 cups unsweetened apple juice
  or cider
1 slice orange
1 cinnamon stick
2 whole cardamom pods
1 ½ cups Arborio rice

TOPPINGS

½ cup heavy cream
1 teaspoon granulated sugar
½ teaspoon rum (optional)
¼ cup almonds or walnuts,
  toasted and coarsely chopped

*

HOT BUTTERED
RUM SAUCE
....

1 cup packed brown sugar
½ cup dark rum
½ cup heavy cream
4 tablespoons (½ stick)
unsalted butter, chilled and
cut into pieces

Whisk the brown sugar in a heavy, small saucepan over medium heat until melted and smooth. Pour in the rum and cream and simmer, stirring until the sauce is smooth, thickened, and reduced to about ¾ cup, about 30 minutes. Whisk in the butter until melted. This sauce can be prepared ahead and kept for several hours at room temperature or refrigerated overnight. Reheat before serving.

Use this with Mulled Cider and Rum Risotto and Floating Islands with Melted Chocolate Morsels (page 37). Or simply eat with a spoon.

*

To make the risotto, melt 4 tablespoons of the butter in a large, heavy nonstick skillet over medium heat. Add the apples and sugar and cook, stirring occasionally, until the apples are just tender, 6 to 7 minutes. Pour the rum in at the edge of the skillet. Heat briefly, then ignite it carefully using a long match. Shake the skillet until the flame goes out. Stir in the vanilla. Set aside.

Bring the apple juice, orange slice, and spices to a simmer in a medium saucepan. Melt the remaining butter in a large, heavy nonstick saucepan over medium-low heat. Add the rice to the melted butter and stir for 2 minutes, or until the rice starts to become translucent. Pour in about ¾ cup spiced apple juice and bring it to a boil, stirring. Lower the heat to a point where the liquid is simmering gently. Stir continually until the liquid is completely absorbed. Stir in the cooked apple mixture and an additional ½ cup spiced apple juice. Stir until the liquid is absorbed. Continue adding the spiced apple juice ½ cup at a time at first, then ¼ cup at a time toward the end of cooking, stirring until each addition is absorbed. Cook, adjusting the heat as necessary so the liquid always simmers gently, until the rice is tender but not mushy, 20 to 25 minutes total. You may not end up using all the liquid.

Whip the cream in the chilled bowl of a stand mixer fitted with the whisk attachment, adding the sugar little by little and then the rum, if desired.

To serve, spoon the warm risotto into soup bowls. Top it with whipped cream and sprinkle it with nuts.

Pavlova with Pinot Noir Strawberries

This dessert honors two women: the great Russian ballerina Anna Pavlova and my mother, Muguette Richard. Supposedly, the Pavlova—a baked meringue with a little vinegar and cornstarch—was invented by the Australians as one of a number of chefs' creations dedicated to Ms. Pavlova, whose performances electrified Australian audiences in 1929. It is often served with a red fruit compote or sauce, so I thought why not try the traditional macerated strawberries that my mom used to make for us in France? I think both the grand ballerina and my mom would take this as a compliment. At least I hope so.   ✳ SERVES 4

PAVLOVA

4 egg whites

1 cup granulated sugar

1 teaspoon white vinegar

1 teaspoon vanilla extract

1 ½ tablespoons cornstarch

PINOT NOIR STRAWBERRIES
AND WHIPPED CREAM

14 mint leaves

1 pound strawberries, trimmed,
    washed, and cut into quarters

½ cup packed brown sugar, dark

1 cup Pinot Noir red wine

2 cinnamon sticks

Zest from 1 lemon

1 teaspoon vanilla extract

1 star anise

2 tablespoons crème de cassis
    (optional)

½ cup heavy cream

1 tablespoon granulated sugar

Preheat the oven to 250 degrees.

Put the egg whites in the bowl of a stand mixer fitted with the whisk attachment and beat on high for about 1 minute, until the whites are foamy. Add the sugar 1 tablespoon at a time and continue whipping for 5 minutes until soft peaks form. Using a rubber spatula, fold in the vinegar, vanilla, and cornstarch.

Line a sheet pan with a piece of parchment paper. Pour the whipped egg whites into the center of the sheet pan. Using your imagination and a rubber spatula, push and poke the meringue, sculpturing it to resemble a modern art porcupine or whatever suits your fancy. Think about making pockets for fruit and cream. Bake for 1 hour and 15 minutes. The result will be a crispy meringue on the outside with a soft and chewy interior. Allow it to cool completely. (At this point, you can keep the meringue for 2 to 3 days at room temperature in a covered container.)

Meanwhile, chop 6 of the mint leaves and set the remaining 8 aside.

In a medium glass or ceramic bowl, stir together chopped mint, strawberries, brown sugar, wine, cinnamon, lemon zest, vanilla, anise, and cassis, if you are using it. Refrigerate until well chilled.

Whip the cream in the chilled bowl of a stand mixer fitted with the whisk attachment, adding the sugar little by little until firm. Transfer to a clean bowl and refrigerate.

Place portions of Pavlova into individual serving dishes and spoon strawberries and whipped cream on top. Decorate each serving with 2 of the reserved whole mint leaves.

Pistachio Linzer Tarts with Fresh Raspberries

I have always thought that the Linzer tart was a good idea, but something about it left me unsatisfied. I don't like the thick, goopy layer of raspberry jam in the middle of the traditional cookie. Here, I use fresh raspberries on a very thin layer of jam. When you bite down, the fresh fruit juice mixes with the sweet, nutty cookie. Also, in a departure from the hazelnut- or almond-based dough that you may be familiar with, I find that ground pistachios contribute a browned-butter note and add an appealing pale green color. * MAKES 6 SMALL TARTS

LINZER DOUGH
⅔ cup granulated sugar
½ cup shelled pistachios
2 teaspoons cinnamon
2 cups all-purpose flour
1 cup (2 sticks) unsalted butter,
    chilled and chopped
1 egg

TOPPING
6 tablespoons raspberry jam
    with seeds
3 half-pint baskets fresh raspberries
Powdered sugar for dusting

Place the sugar, pistachios, cinnamon, and flour in a food processor and pulse until the nuts are finely ground. Add the butter and process until the mixture is the texture of coarse meal. Add the egg and process until the dough is crumbly and moistened, but does not yet form a ball. Pinch a piece of the dough. If it is too dry to hold together, add water, 1 tablespoon at a time, until the dough is evenly moist. Turn it out onto a piece of plastic wrap and form it into a flat rectangle. Wrap and refrigerate for at least 30 minutes. (The dough can keep in the refrigerator for several days.)

To form the cookies, line two large sheet pans with parchment paper. This dough is fragile, so you will work with it cold. Roll the dough out between two large pieces of plastic wrap into a 12-by-16-inch rectangle about ¼ inch thick. Using a 5-inch bowl or plate as a guide and a small, sharp, floured knife, cut out 6 circles. Place the cookies on the sheet pans using a spatula and positioning them 1 or 2 inches apart. Cover the sheet pans with plastic wrap and chill them for at least 1 hour.

Preheat the oven to 350 degrees. Place one rack in the upper third of the oven and one in the lower third. Remove the plastic wrap and bake one sheet on the upper rack and one on the lower rack for 20 minutes or until golden brown, swapping the pan positions halfway through the baking time. Cool the tarts completely on the sheet pans, then gently slide a spatula under the cookies to loosen them and transfer them to wire racks, arranging them in a single layer.

To finish the tarts, evenly spread 1 tablespoon raspberry jam on top of each. Cover the jam layer entirely with fresh raspberries and sprinkle the top with powdered sugar.

Raspberry Tartlet with Strawberry Milk Custard

I love the idea of raspberries, but unless you have a raspberry patch in your backyard, it is very hard, even for fancy chefs, to find raspberries that are sweet, juicy, and ripe. They may look perfect in the supermarket display, but in order to pick them and get them to market while they still look pretty, berry farmers often have to harvest their crop before it is fully ripe, as is the case with so many fresh fruits and vegetables. Rather than fight a losing battle against modern farming, I find that turning the raspberries upside down and filling them with berry coulis looks very "pastry shoppish" but is quite easy and yields little explosions of tart sweetness. When I first started to play with this idea, I made it with regular pastry cream, but I found that blending and straining strawberries and milk produces a luscious berry accent that pulls the whole dessert together. ＊ MAKES 8 TARTLETS

¼ recipe (about ½ pound) Puff
    Pastry (page 50)
7 medium strawberries, trimmed
    and washed
1 cup milk
⅓ cup cornstarch
½ cup granulated sugar
4 egg yolks
Red Berry Coulis (page 53)
4 half-pint baskets fresh raspberries
Chopped pistachios (optional)

Preheat the oven to 350 degrees and line a 12-by-16-inch sheet pan with parchment.

Lightly flour a rolling pin and work surface and roll the puff pastry dough to a thickness of ⅛ inch so that it fits the prepared sheet pan. Lay the dough in the pan. With a fork, poke holes all over the dough, including the edges. Place another piece of parchment paper directly on top of the dough and then set another sheet pan over that. Refrigerate the dough for 15 minutes.

Bake the dough, still weighted down by the second sheet pan, for 15 minutes, then remove the pan and parchment paper and continue baking until the pastry is golden brown, about 15 minutes longer.

Meanwhile, place the strawberries and milk in a food processor or blender. Blend on high for a few minutes until the mixture is uniform, then pour it into a large microwave-safe bowl. In a smaller bowl, toss together the cornstarch and sugar, then add the egg yolks and whisk well. Add the yolk mixture to the strawberry milk and whisk well. Microwave on high for 1 minute, whisk vigorously, then continue to microwave for 1-minute intervals, whisking in between, for a total of 5 minutes. The liquid must thicken and start to boil. When it has come to a boil and has thickened, place a piece of plastic wrap directly on top of the custard and refrigerate.

As soon as the puff pastry is golden brown, transfer it (still on the parchment paper) to a cutting board and, with a very sharp knife, carefully cut it into eight 3½-inch squares. (You will have extra pastry that you have trimmed from the edges.) Set the squares aside on a rack to continue cooling.

Place the strawberry custard in the bowl of a stand mixer fitted with the paddle attachment and whip it so it becomes light and fluffy, about 3 minutes. Pour the coulis into a squeeze bottle.

When the pastry squares are cooled, spoon 1 tablespoon of custard onto each square and spread it evenly. Place 16 raspberries, upside down in rows of 4, on each square. Fill each raspberry center with coulis.

To serve, place 1 tablespoon custard in the center of each plate and position the pastry on top of it. Drizzle a little bit of coulis around the tart. Sprinkle with pistachios, if desired.

Puff Pastry

This is perhaps the most magic and wonderful of all doughs. No yeast, and yet it puffs up into a thousand (actually 729) layers. Steam from the butter trying to escape but trapped by the careful folding of the layers is the secret here. It is important to bake this thoroughly, or you will get a chewy, raw mouthful. Your goal is crunch from beginning to end. Traditionalists may be shocked that I call for Wondra flour, but it is easy to work, very tender, and requires no sifting. So why not?

* MAKES ABOUT 2 POUNDS DOUGH

4 cups Wondra flour
2 teaspoons fine sea salt
About 1½ cups ice water
2 cups (4 sticks) unsalted butter,
   very cold

Place the flour and salt in the bowl of a stand mixer fitted with the dough hook. Mixing on low speed, add the water a bit at a time until the dough begins to come together and is sticky but not wet. It is okay if you have water left over. Turn the speed to high and mix for several seconds, or until the dough coheres. If it does not form a single ball, don't worry—you can knead it on the work surface.

Flour a work surface and place the dough on it. Knead briefly, if necessary for the dough to hold together. Form it into a disk about 10 inches in diameter. Using a thin, sharp knife, cut a ¾-by-½-inch X deep into the surface of the dough to help it relax.

Place a 12-inch piece of plastic wrap in a clear space on the work surface. Place the butter in the center of it and cover it with a second piece of plastic wrap. Using a rolling pin, pound the butter into an 8-by-6-inch rectangle. Set aside.

Roll the dough into a 10-by-8-inch rectangle (2 inches larger than the butter on the sides). Place the butter in the center of the dough. Stretch and bring up the sides of the dough, pressing the seams to seal them, so that the dough encases the butter. Flour the dough and gently roll it from front to back into a rectangle about 18 inches long and 10 inches wide. Be careful not to let the butter come through the dough. If the room is warm, the butter may become too soft and break through the surface. If so, stop and refrigerate the dough until the butter hardens again.

Fold up the bottom third of the rectangle to the center, then fold the top third down and over it, as you would fold a letter. Rotate the dough a quarter turn (90 degrees), so that the folded edge is on the left. Roll it out again into an 18-by-10-inch rectangle. Again fold the dough into thirds. Press two fingertips into the dough to indicate that it has been rolled and folded twice. Wrap the dough in plastic wrap and refrigerate it for at least 45 minutes.

Return the chilled dough to the floured surface, again with the folded edge to the left. With a rolling pin, press down on the edge closest to you and then on the far end, to seal the dough before rolling. Roll and fold the dough as before, then turn it and repeat a fourth time. Mark the top with four fingers and refrigerate for at least another 45 minutes.

Roll and fold the dough two more times as described. Mark it with six fingers and refrigerate it again for at least 45 minutes, or up to 5 days. If you want to freeze the dough, cut it into the desired portions, roll it out ½ inch thick, wrap it well, and freeze it for up to 1 month. Defrost the dough overnight in the refrigerator before using.

Soaked (but Not Soggy) Sponge Cake

When I was a young boy, France was still recovering from the war. Small-town pastry shops couldn't afford refrigerated showcases, and without refrigeration, gelatin will melt after a few hours. Any lovely pastry made with it would look very sad—like a pretty little girl who got caught in the rain in a party dress. The only chefs who used gelatin were restaurant chefs with plenty of refrigerator space.

By the time I went to work for Mr. Lenôtre, pastry shops had begun to compete with each other for the beauty of their desserts, and refrigerated showcases had come into common use, making it possible for us to use gelatin. Now we could make mousses out of fresh fruit; we could replace egg yolks and buttercreams with lighter gelatin mousses and meringues. But one thing we could not replace—or should I say, I had not yet figured out how to replace—was the simple syrup that we used to soak our layer cakes. You need a ton of sugar to make syrup thick enough to soak into a cake. To my taste, the result is overly sweet. The problem is, if you use less sugar, the syrup is less thick, and the cake that you soak in the evening will be sitting in a puddle of syrup the next morning.

Trying to make a virtue of necessity, pastry chefs would lace their soaking syrups with rum or kirsch or other sweet booze. I agree that it makes you feel nice to have a little drink, and I think for some of those chefs, it was a case of "one ounce of rum for the cake and one sip for me." But in desserts, as in life, you can't solve a problem by drowning it in alcohol.

I took my first step in my search for the Holy Grail of infusing flavor nearly thirty years ago. One day I was making apple aspic, but I was in a rush, so after cooking the whole apples, skin, seeds, and all, I strained them, placed the pureed apples in a bowl over ice, and started whisking

*

RED BERRY COULIS

....

½ pound fresh or frozen raspberries or strawberries
4 ounces brown sugar, light

Place the berries in a blender with the sugar and blend on high until well pureed, 1 or 2 minutes. Pour the puree through a fine-mesh strainer and reserve it in a bowl. Keeps up to 3 days in the refrigerator, covered.

*

the mixture to speed up the cooling process. I noted a change in the texture of the mixture. The apple puree was looking more and more like apple meringue rather than apple aspic. I realized the pectin in the apples works just like gelatin to create a mousselike texture. The next step seems simple in retrospect, but it wasn't for another ten years that I had the idea of whipping fruit juice and gelatin over a bowl of ice. The result was a deliciously airy and fruity whipped cream . . . without the cream.

I wish I could say a lightbulb blazed in my brain. But it was more like a little flashlight. I didn't see any practical use for this discovery in my pastry shop because if my customers bought something made with gelatin, it may have looked pretty in my showcase, but it would probably melt if you put it on the backseat of a car in sunny Santa Fe or Los Angeles.

Still, I persevered. My *petit* flashlight became a little brighter when I had my own restaurant, Citrus, in Los Angeles. One day I made a lighter version of *poires belle Hélène*. Instead of ice cream, I served a puree of pear and gelatin that I whipped over ice. It was creamy like ice cream but no butter, no eggs.

The answer to my soaking issue was right in front of my eyes, but I still soaked my layer cakes with simple syrup, not realizing I had already solved the problem of how to soak without making cake overly sweet and wet.

The hundred-watt lightbulb went off the day I took the juice (but not the pulp) of beautiful sweet oranges, mixed it with gelatin, and poured it over a sponge cake. I put it in the fridge and—voilà!—the next day I ate a delicious mouthful of cake infused with moist (but *not* wet) texture, full of orange flavor, and just sweet enough. I was expecting something nice, but this was perfection!

On that day I said *au revoir* forever to simple syrup.

✳ SERVES 8

Sponge Cake (page 56)

1 quart pulp-free orange juice

½ cup sugar

6 teaspoons (3 packages) unflavored gelatin

1 pound strawberries, washed, trimmed, and halved

1 cup heavy cream

2 tablespoons sugar

Red Berry Coulis (page 53) or

    Hot Chocolate Sauce (page 59)

Make the sponge cake and set it aside to cool while you make the soaking syrup: Pour the orange juice into a saucepan, add sugar and gelatin, and whisk to dissolve. Bring the mixture to a boil, then let it cool for 30 minutes.

When the cake is cool, cover the entire top with strawberries, placing them cut sides up or down, or alternating for a decorative pattern. Pour three quarters of the warm orange gelatin over the cake, soaking the strawberries as well. Refrigerate for 1 hour. When the gelatin on the cake has set, reheat the remaining soaking sauce and pour it over the strawberries and cake. Refrigerate again before serving, about 1 hour.

Whip the cream in the chilled bowl of a stand mixer fitted with the whisk attachment, adding the sugar little by little until firm. Transfer to a clean bowl and refrigerate.

Serve the sponge cake chilled. Spoon it into small bowls and add a dollop of whipped cream and a drizzling of coulis or chocolate sauce.

Sponge Cake (Genoise)

Sponge cake in pastry making fills the same role that bread does in a sandwich. It is a platform (and a roof) for other recipe components such as mousses, pastry creams, and ganaches. Made with three simple ingredients, this cake gets its volume from the air suspended in the batter without requiring any other leavening. Its slightly dry texture permits it to take on a variety of interesting tastes when soaked with flavored syrup.

In the old days, we made sponge cake over a double boiler, or bain-marie, and we whipped and added butter to the mixture. I don't like that. Butter is unnecessary, and removing it produces a lighter result. In most desserts there is already enough fat in the other components. Adding butter here reminds me of the way some people butter their croissants—which are already loaded with butter to begin with.

About twenty years ago, I decided to skip the bain-marie and found no loss in quality but a big reduction in time-consuming labor. I add all kinds of flavoring to my sponge cake—dried, powdered raspberries, ground almonds, cocoa powder, instant coffee. And most recently, I have pretty much abandoned traditional soaking syrups and begun to use gelatin with fruit juices, as in my Soaked (but Not Soggy) Sponge Cake on page 53.

   2 tablespoons unsalted butter
   ¾ cup plus 2 tablespoons
      all-purpose flour
   4 eggs
   ½ cup sugar

Preheat the oven to 325 degrees.

Refrigerate a 9-by-2-inch round baking pan. Place the butter in the microwave on high for 5 seconds until it is just starting to melt but is still solid. Use a pastry brush to coat the inner surface of the chilled pan with the creamy butter. Add 2 tablespoons of the flour to the baking pan, rotating the pan to fully coat the bottom. Then, holding the pan over the sink, tap the flour onto the sides to cover the entire surface. Turn the pan upside down and tap the bottom to release any loose flour into the sink.

Place the eggs in the bowl of a stand mixer fitted with the whisk attachment and whisk on high for about 1 minute, until the eggs are foamy. Add the sugar 1 tablespoon at a time and continue to whip for 10 minutes on high. Remove the bowl from the mixer and, using a rubber spatula, gently fold in the remaining ¾ cup flour one third at a time, gently folding between each addition. Mix until the flour is just incorporated. Pour the batter into the prepared pan and bake for 30 minutes. Let the cake cool in the pan for 10 minutes, then turn it out and set it upright on a wire rack to continue cooling.

Choco-Mocha Layer Cake with Marshmallow Buttercream

Mocha is the offspring of the marriage of two plain-looking beans: coffee and cacao. In their natural states, both are very bitter, and I wonder what culinary adventurer had the courage to eat them in the first place. The depth of flavor they acquire when roasted, however, is simply wonderful, and maybe because of that very bitterness, they go well with lots of sugar—the ingredient common to all desserts.

The cakey part of this layer cake is mixed with instant (powdered) espresso, which gives it a nutty, toasted taste. Likewise, I put coffee in my marshmallow buttercream and in that way introduce a flavor theme that unites the cream layers and the cake layers. You'll notice there are no egg yolks and not very much butter in the buttercream, while the marshmallow is nothing more than gelatinized egg whites and sugar. The result is lighter than buttercream but more intense than marshmallow. Soaking the sponge cake with gelatin infuses and moistens the cake with sweet coffee flavor but has none of the wetness and oversweetness of simple syrup to weigh it down.   * SERVES 10

GENOISE AND SOAKING SYRUP
Sponge Cake (page 56),
    made with 1 teaspoon instant
    coffee added to the flour
2 cups coffee
¼ cup sugar
3 teaspoons unflavored gelatin

MARSHMALLOW BUTTERCREAM FILLING

4 egg whites

¼ cup sugar

1 teaspoon instant espresso powder

2 teaspoons unflavored gelatin

2 tablespoons water

½ cup (1 stick) unsalted butter,
    room temperature

Hot Chocolate Sauce (opposite)

The day before you need to serve the dessert, bake the genoise, making sure to add the coffee powder. After cooling the cake for 10 minutes, transfer it from the pan to a wire rack and cool it completely. Wrap it in plastic and refrigerate. The next day, dampen the bottom of the clean cake pan and place an 18-inch piece of plastic wrap in the bottom. Cut the genoise horizontally into equal layers. Place the top half upside down in the cake pan.

Make the soaking syrup by mixing the coffee, sugar, and gelatin with a wire whisk. Place in a microwave-safe bowl and cook for 1 minute or until the gelatin is dissolved. Let the syrup sit for 5 minutes, then spoon half of it over the bottom of the cake, thoroughly soaking it. Set aside.

To make the buttercream, place the egg whites in the bowl of a stand mixer fitted with the whisk attachment and beat on high for about 1 minute, until the whites are foamy. Add the sugar 1 tablespoon at a time and continue mixing for about 10 minutes until the egg whites are stiff. While the egg whites are whipping, place the espresso powder, gelatin, and water in a small microwave-safe bowl and heat on high in the microwave for 30

HOT CHOCOLATE SAUCE

2 cups (12 ounces) bittersweet or semisweet chocolate, finely chopped (or chocolate chips)

1 cup heavy cream

2 tablespoons apricot liqueur, amaretto, or rum

Combine the chocolate, cream, and liqueur in the top of a double boiler over gently simmering water. Melt until smooth, stirring constantly. Keep warm over the simmering water if serving immediately, otherwise remove from the heat, pour into a covered container, and refrigerate. When ready to serve, reheat in the double boiler.

seconds to melt the gelatin; set the mixture aside for 5 minutes. When the egg whites are whipped, add the coffee-and-gelatin mix to the bowl and whip for a few seconds until combined.

Place the butter in the microwave for a few seconds until it just starts to melt. In a large bowl, using a whisk, blend the butter until it has the consistency of mayonnaise. Using a rubber spatula, gently fold the egg white mixture into the butter.

Spoon the filling onto the soaked bottom cake layer, spreading it to the edges of the pan. Add the second cake layer cut side up (this allows the soaking liquid to be well absorbed) and spoon the remaining soaking liquid onto the cake. Cover the exposed surface of the cake with plastic wrap. Refrigerate it for at least 2 hours.

Remove the cake from the refrigerator at least 1 hour before serving and transfer it to a serving plate of your choice. Serve the slices with chocolate sauce drizzled on top.

Maple Parsnip Cake with Maple Meringue Frosting

Back in the 1980s, one of the most influential American cookbook writers was the late Sheila Lukins. Her *Silver Palate Cookbook* and its companion volume, *The New Basics*, drew on her experience from her revolutionary take-out shop, the Silver Palate. One of the go-to desserts was the carrot cake by her mom, Berta. I liked the idea of using a humble root vegetable as the basis for a dessert treat too.

Now, if carrots are humble, then parsnips are surely among the poorest peasants in the entire Duchy of Vegetables. Poor Monsieur Parsnip! He doesn't even have the happy orange color that brightens the carrot. But when cooked, parsnips have a flavor and consistency that reminds me of the sweetest roast chestnuts. Grating them gives the cake the mouthfeel of shredded coconut. Add maple syrup for earthy sweetness and aromatic spices, and you have a lovely cake that has one other special quality; if you ask the people around your table what is in it, no one will ever be able to guess. ✳ SERVES 8

CAKE

2 cups almond meal (or very finely
    ground almonds)*
¾ cup all-purpose flour
1 teaspoon baking soda
2 teaspoons ground cinnamon
¼ teaspoon fine sea salt
1 cup maple syrup

---

* Freeze the almonds before grinding them.

8 tablespoons (1 stick) unsalted
   butter, melted
2 eggs
3 teaspoons fresh ginger, grated
2 cups packed parsnips, peeled and
   finely grated (about 6 medium)
½ cup toasted pecans

MAPLE MERINGUE FROSTING
1 cup maple syrup
4 egg whites
2 tablespoons sugar

Position a rack in the center of the oven and preheat to 350 degrees.

Butter the bottom of a 9-inch round cake pan, line it with a piece of parchment paper cut to fit, then butter and flour the paper and the sides of the pan.

To make the cake, combine the dry ingredients in a bowl. In the bowl of a stand mixer fitted with the paddle attachment, beat the maple syrup, butter, and eggs on medium speed until well combined, scraping the sides of the bowl as needed. Add the dry mixture, 1 cup at a time, until just combined. Stir in the ginger and parsnips. Pour the batter into the prepared pan.

Arrange the pecans in a decorative pattern on top of the cake. Bake for 40 minutes, or until the cake is golden brown and a skewer inserted in the center comes out clean. Transfer the pan to a wire rack and cool for 20 minutes.

While the cake is baking, make the frosting: Pour the maple syrup into a medium saucepan. Place the egg whites in the bowl of a stand mixer fitted with the whisk attachment. Set the maple syrup over medium heat and, using a candy thermometer, monitor its temperature. When it reaches 230 degrees, start to whip the eggs on high speed. After about 4 minutes, add the sugar to the egg whites. Once the maple syrup reaches 252 degrees, pour it into the whites in a slow, steady stream as close to the side of the bowl as possible to avoid splattering. Continue mixing on medium speed until the bottom of the mixing bowl is cool to the touch, about 15 minutes.

Loosen the sides of the cake with a knife and remove it from the pan. Let it cool completely on a rack. Serve the cake dolloped with the maple meringue.

Piña Colada Cake

My wife, Laurence, and I ate dinner at a friend's house some years ago, and for dessert we had one of the moistest, creamiest cakes we had ever tasted. It lives in her memory, levitated on a fluffy cloud of milk mixture. And so, because my wife loved it and I love her, I have created my own version of that cake. I have added coconut for taste and texture, pineapple juice for freshness, and gelatin to the soaking syrup to keep the cake from getting too soggy. Make it on a cold winter night, and see if it doesn't transport you to the tropics. ✳ SERVES 8

CAKE

¼ cup shredded unsweetened coconut
¼ cup powdered sugar
4 eggs
⅓ cup granulated sugar
¼ cup Wondra flour

SOAKING SYRUP

1 cup sweetened coconut milk
    (such as Coco Lopez brand)
1½ cups pineapple juice
4 teaspoons (2 envelopes) unflavored
    gelatin
½ cup dark rum

WHIPPED CREAM

1 cup heavy cream
2 tablespoons granulated sugar

To make the cake, preheat the oven to 350 degrees. Butter and flour a 9-inch round cake pan. Pulse the coconut and powdered sugar in a blender or food processor until finely ground; set aside.

Place the eggs in the bowl of a stand mixer fitted with the whisk attachment and beat on high for about 1 minute, until they are foamy. Add the sugar 1 tablespoon at a time and whip for 10 minutes on high speed. Using a rubber spatula, gently fold in the flour and the reserved coconut sugar. Mix just until the flour is incorporated. Pour the batter into the prepared pan and bake for 40 minutes until the cake pulls away from the side of the pan and springs back when touched. Let the cake cool in the pan for 30 minutes.

While the cake is baking and cooling, prepare the soaking syrup. Combine the coconut milk and pineapple juice in a medium saucepan. Bring the mixture to a boil and remove it from the heat. Add the gelatin, stirring until dissolved. Stir in the rum and allow the syrup to cool to room temperature.

After cake has cooled, cut off the "bump" from the top to make a level surface. Place the cake in a quiche mold or other 10-inch high-edged pan larger than the cake itself. Slowly pour the soaking syrup over the cake. Refrigerate it for about 30 minutes, then, using a baster, suck up any syrup that oozed out of the cake and drizzle it back onto it.

Whip the cream in the bowl of a stand mixer fitted with the whisk attachment, adding the sugar little by little until firm. Transfer to a clean bowl and refrigerate.

Chill the cake completely and serve it with a dollop of whipped cream.

Apricot Chocolate Layer Cake

Some figures of speech are instantly seductive. I don't know exactly why, but the term "flourless chocolate cake" is one of them. Don't be so easily seduced. Many cakes with this attractive name are sad to look at, like a dark, collapsed soufflé—a pastry chef's version of the black hole that eats galaxies at the end of the universe. Even Julia Child's version could not defy the laws of gravity. This layer cake derives structure from the starch in rice flour, so I guess I can't call it flourless; but *wheatless* doesn't do much for me as a word. The batter is, in fact, nothing more than classic French *biscuits cuillères* made with rice flour. Butter and apricots combine in a heavenly, rich sauce that has an almond hint from the ground dried apricot pits in the amaretto cookies.

Note: Plan in advance. You need to soak the apricots for a full day and then let the assembled cake sit overnight for the flavors to meld.   * SERVES 10

CAKE AND FILLING

1 pound dried apricots

5 eggs, separated

1 cup plus 2 tablespoons sugar

1 pound plus 3 ounces bittersweet
   chocolate, chopped

4 tablespoons (½ stick) unsalted
   butter, cut into pieces

⅔ cup rice flour

¼ cup cocoa powder (Dutch process)

APRICOT COULIS

12 fresh, ripe apricots, washed, halved,
   and pitted (or 12 dried apricots
   reconstituted in the orange juice)

¾ cup packed brown sugar, light

¼ cup orange juice, plus more
   if needed
6 amaretto cookies (such as Lazzaroni-
   brand Amaretti di Saronno)

The night before you make the cake, place the dried apricots
into a medium bowl and pour enough water over them to just
cover. Soak overnight.

Preheat the oven to 350 degrees. Butter an 8-by-2-inch
springform pan.

Place the rehydrated apricots, with their soaking liquid, in
a blender and blend on high to make a very smooth puree. Set
aside.

Place the egg yolks with half of the sugar in the bowl of a
stand mixer fitted with the whisk attachment and beat on high
speed for 5 minutes, until light yellow and creamy.

While the yolks are whipping, place 3 ounces of the chocolate and the butter in a microwave-safe bowl and microwave on
high at 30-second intervals, stirring in between, until just
melted. Add this chocolate mixture, along with ½ cup of the
apricot puree, to the whipped yolks and mix by hand with a
whisk. Transfer to another bowl. Wash and dry the mixer bowl
and whisk attachment.

Place the egg whites into the clean bowl of the stand mixer
fitted again with the whisk attachment and beat on high for
about 1 minute, until the whites are foamy. Add the remaining
sugar 1 tablespoon at a time until soft peaks begin to form.
Whisk for 10 minutes, until the whites are glossy and firm.

While the egg whites are whipping, sift the rice flour and
cocoa powder together.

Remove the egg whites from the stand mixer. Add the yolk-and-chocolate mixture and the sifted rice flour and cocoa powder and incorporate all ingredients gently, using a rubber spatula.

Pour the batter into the prepared pan and bake for 40 minutes, or until a cake tester inserted in the center comes out clean. Let the cake cool overnight in the pan.

While the cake bakes, make the filling: Place the remaining pound of chocolate in a microwave-safe bowl and microwave it on high at 30-second intervals, stirring in between, until melted. Once the chocolate is melted, add 2½ cups of the apricot puree and whisk until smooth. (If any apricot remains, reserve it for another use.) Cover with plastic wrap and refrigerate overnight.

The next day, place the chocolate filling in the bowl of a stand mixer fitted with a wire whisk attachment and whip on medium speed for 3 minutes, until it is a spreadable consistency.

Unmold the cake. Wash the springform pan and place it on a clean sheet pan, without its bottom. Using a serrated knife, carefully slice the cake horizontally into three layers. Place the top slice into the bottom of the pan. Spoon one-third of the filling on top of the cake and spread it evenly with the back of a spoon or a rubber spatula. Place the second cake layer into the mold and spread on another third of the filling. Place the last layer on top, spoon on the remaining filling, and spread it into an even coating. Refrigerate the whole cake for 2 hours.

Make the apricot coulis by placing the apricots, brown sugar, orange juice, and amaretto cookies in a blender or food processor and blending on high for 1 minute. The mixture should have the consistency of applesauce. If it is too thick, add a little more orange juice. Set aside.

To unmold the cake, wrap the outside of the pan with a warm, damp towel to help loosen the chocolate. Carefully unlatch the springform mechanism. With the help of a large metal offset spatula, place the cake on your serving dish. Cut slices and drizzle them with apricot coulis. Serve with additional sauce on the plate.

Sweet Tomato Basil Tart

Once the word *gourmet* had been coined, it inaugurated a never-ending march of silly food trends. I suppose as long as there are people who want to have "the next great thing," it will surely continue. Today we have deconstructed/reconstructed molecular food that may appear as insane to future food historians as an alchemist's manual would look to us. In the 1970s, nouvelle cuisine conceived of the innovation of using words from one part of a menu in another part. Thus we got Swordfish Chops, Strawberry Consommé, Lamb Sushi, maybe even Tenderloin of Turnip. Still, I applaud the sense of adventure of chefs who are willing to explore any and every combination. This is a long way of saying I decided to put a nouvelle homage of my own in this book: a dessert made of sweetened ripe tomatoes, puff pastry, and a sweet basil meringue.

Note: This dessert can be assembled in a few minutes, if you have the puff pastry on hand in the freezer and roast the tomatoes and prepare the tomato jam the day before. ＊ SERVES 8

TOMATO TART

10 Roma tomatoes, peeled*
¼ cup granulated sugar
½ recipe (about 1 pound) Puff Pastry
   (page 50)
1 egg, beaten
½ cup packed brown sugar
Juice from 1 lime
½ teaspoon vanilla extract
1 tablespoon cornstarch

---

*   To peel a tomato, cut a small x in the bottom of the tomato and submerge it in boiling water for 30 seconds. The skin can then easily be removed.

3 egg whites

8 leaves sweet basil, washed and
   dried

¼ cup granulated sugar

Preheat the oven to 200 degrees.

Cut a 1-inch section from the middle of 8 of the peeled tomatoes, then slice each of these sections into 4 uniform ¼-inch
rounds. Set them aside. Seed and finely dice the trimmings from
the 8 tomatoes and all of the remaining 2 tomatoes (you need
about 1 cup) and set the dice aside for the jam.

Place the 32 tomato rounds on a sheet pan lined with Silpat
or parchment. Sprinkle the granulated sugar on top of the
rounds. Bake for 1½ hours. Cool the tomato rounds completely
in the pan, cover them with plastic wrap, and leave them at cool
room temperature. (This step can be done the day before.)

Increase the oven temperature to 350 degrees.

Roll the puff pastry out ⅛ inch thick and cut out a 6-by-16-
inch rectangle. Place the pastry on a sheet pan lined with Silpat
or parchment and refrigerate for 10 minutes. Brush the beaten
egg in a 1-inch strip down each long side of the rectangle. Make a
lip by folding these long edges in on each side, pressing with your
finger so they stick well. The dough rectangle will now measure
4 by 16 inches. Place it in the freezer for 10 minutes, then,
holding the rectangle by the short ends, flip the entire thing over
so the folded edges are underneath, effectively becoming a
stand. Brush beaten egg in a 1-inch strip along each long side as
you did before. Prick the center of the tart with a fork, and then
bake it for 25 minutes. Rotate the pan in the oven and reduce

the oven temperature to 325 degrees. Bake for 20 minutes longer, until golden brown.

While the shell is baking, make tomato jam: Combine the reserved diced tomatoes, brown sugar, lime juice, vanilla, and cornstarch in a small saucepan and bring the mixture to a boil over high heat. Reduce the heat to medium and simmer for 5 minutes, stirring occasionally.

When the tart shell is baked and slightly cooled, spread the tomato jam down the center, leaving about ½ inch clean on the two long sides. Starting at one end of the shell, place 4 of the reserved tomato rounds in a row, overlapping them slightly. Repeat until all the rounds have been used.

To make the meringue, place the egg whites and basil in a blender. Process on high for a few seconds. Transfer the mixture to a stand mixer fitted with the whisk attachment and whip on high, adding the granulated sugar 1 tablespoon at a time. Whip until hard peaks form, 5 to 7 minutes. Spoon the meringue on top of the tomatoes to cover. Using the back of the spoon, "lift" the meringue to form decorative jagged spikes on the surface.

Preheat the oven to broil and place a rack in the center.

Broil the tart until the meringue is golden—but stay close and keep an eye on it. If the tips burn a bit, it is okay. Alternatively, you can use a blowtorch for this step, if you have one. Let the tart rest for 10 minutes before using a serrated knife to cut it into slices.

Tip: To make cleaner cuts, keep a glass of hot water next to you and clean off the knife blade between slices.

PART II

You Can Take the
Frenchman Out
of France, but . . .

I have been an American citizen for ten years, but inside I still have a very French brain. There is no question that my basic techniques are the ones I learned in France, and I could not think of doing a book of desserts without paying homage to the ones I loved first. Fixed in the golden glow of childhood memory, they are like mother's milk to me (and, come to think of it, like my mother's butter and jam and fruit compote). Some I have re-created without changing a thing (Cherry Clafouti, page 92); others I have adapted, always paying heed to my first law of cuisine— add flavor, subtract heaviness. My Praline Cake with Buttercream Mousse (page 119) has much less sugar than Mr. Lenôtre's. The cake roll for my Christmas log (page 112) contains no flour. My version of the napoleon (Crème Brûlée Sandwich, page 109) is made with phyllo instead of the more laborious puff pastry. But all of these desserts would be recognizable to a Frenchman who had never set foot in America. They have a French feeling to them.

The use of pastry bags and piping is widely known in France, and I definitely brought that over with me. As an apprentice, I probably piped more than I performed any other task in every shop I worked in. American dessert recipes tend to shy away from piping, but as you see in many of the desserts in this book, it gives a bewitching and uniform shape to ladyfingers and éclairs, and I can't imagine a better way to introduce fillings into cream puffs (page 104) or a layer cake.

Precision and technique really define the culinary legacy of the French kitchen. Whether you are whipping whole eggs in France or egg whites and gelatin in America, you are whipping, using the same tools, looking for the same results. Whether you are cooking Italian food, Mexican food, or French food, many of the methods and tools used in modern kitchens all over the world were developed in the eighteenth and nineteenth centuries in France, when everyday cooking evolved into the art of cuisine.

Unquestionably, French pastry chefs sometimes seem as concerned with the look of their desserts as they are with the taste and texture. Attractiveness is a good thing, although in the hands of some aggressively modern chefs, it might appear that their first goal is to make a unique graphic statement even if that gets in the way of a great recipe. Still, the neatness and symmetry of a charlotte (page 94) and the winding sugar spiral of a Cinnabun (my version of the classic *bolux*, see page 85) are intrinsically beautiful.

My use of nuts in doughs and batters comes directly out of the French dessert tradition. I have been adding nuts to recipes—or thinking about adding them—since I took up my first spatula and whisk. Because nuts have no gluten, and therefore virtually no ability to expand (that is the chief virtue of wheat flour), you cannot always simply substitute almonds for flour. But if you don't need dough that expands a lot, try nuts, particularly almonds.

I love the flavor of almonds. It has a sweet component, a bitter component (which you might think odd for pastry, but bitterness calls out for its mate, sweetness), and a buttery, earthy accent.

My preference for almonds has something to do with the inescapable fact that there are some foods that are perfect for what they do. Sure, there are shortenings other than butter. And, yes, there are binders and emulsifiers other than eggs. But in dessert making, something about the big, round flavors and textures embracing and enhancing the effect of sweetness explains my fondness for almonds.

In France, through good examples and bad, I learned the primary importance of ingredients. Today, I would never serve the margarine croissants that we made with Mr. Sauvage. But the special butter that Mr. Lenôtre bought—I still have not found its equal anywhere in the world. The explosion in fine dining and health consciousness is now a worldwide phenomenon, but when I arrived in America, you would have been hard-pressed to find the tremendous variety of fresh fruits and vegetables that are more and more available. And *organic* was a word more often applied to waste material than to food.

In France, I learned that the most important unit of time in planning any recipe is the season. Fruits and vegetables in season cannot be surpassed; out of season, they always need help. You cannot put the warmth of June that makes delicious strawberries or the crisp coolness of October that ripens apples in a can. Human ingenuity can never coax flavor out of ingredients like the nurturing hand of Mother Nature.

When I say that the methods and tools of modern cuisine are French, that doesn't mean that if it's French it's good, and if it's not French it's not as good. It just means that all chefs share a common culinary language that has its roots in France.

But it is more than that—there is a smell or, should I say (more genteelly), an aroma on streets in France where things are being baked. It is a perfume of butter, sugar, eggs, fruit. It is a sweet spirit, wholly French, and it inhabits my soul.

Apple Compote Tart

My mother was a good cook, but you wouldn't call her the most fabulous cook in France. Raising a houseful of kids mostly on her own was enough of a challenge, without throwing *ooh-la-la* gourmet cooking into the mix. Still, like most of us who look back on our earlier years, I find there are things Maman made that conjure up sweet memories of childhood or, more to the point, memories of childhood sweets.

Like most mothers in France, she was well versed in the art of *chausson aux pommes*, a simple applesauce tart with a pastry crust. I would come home after school, drop off my books, and grab one of these tarts as I ran to play football (soccer).

This recipe is inspired by that tart of my childhood, but I have called for brown sugar and cinnamon, two ingredients that I rarely used until I came to America. And rather than a flaky pastry crust baked in single-serving portions, I make a larger tart with a fluffy, moist brioche dough and an almond-and-brown-sugar topping.

I hope this makes your children happy football players or happy at whatever they chose to do after school.   *   SERVES 8

APPLE TART

½ recipe (1 ¼ pounds) Brioche Dough
   (page 81)
6 Fuji apples, peeled, cored, and
   cut into ½-inch dice (6 cups)
¾ cup packed brown sugar, dark
1 teaspoon cinnamon
1 cup heavy cream
1½ teaspoons granulated sugar
¼ cup water

⅓ cup sliced almonds
⅓ cup packed brown sugar, dark
2 egg whites

Preheat the oven to 375 degrees. To make the tart, butter the inside of a 10-inch quiche mold or springform pan. Lightly flour a work surface and the top of the dough and roll it out to about a 10-inch circle. Press the dough into the bottom of the pan. Cover the mold and dough with plastic wrap and set aside to rest.

Meanwhile, make the filling. Place the apples into a large pot with the brown sugar and cinnamon. Cover and cook slowly on medium heat for 15 minutes, stirring occasionally. Continue cooking, uncovered, for 5 minutes longer, stirring once or twice. Add the heavy cream and cook for 5 minutes, stirring every once in a while. Transfer the apples to a bowl and cool them on the counter.

Pour the cooled apple mixture into the center of the dough circle and spread it carefully, leaving a ½-inch border around the perimeter of the dough. In a small bowl, stir together the granulated sugar and water. Brush the mixture onto the border. Bake for 10 minutes. The dough will rise up along the edge of the pan as it bakes.

While the tart is baking, mix together the almonds, brown sugar, and egg whites to make the topping. Once the tart has baked for 10 minutes, carefully spoon and spread the topping over the apple compote to cover it. Return the tart to the oven and bake it for 15 minutes longer. Cool before serving.

Brioche Dough

Brioche is more of a bread dough than a pastry dough. Maybe that's why my father, who was a bread baker, made it. I never tasted his (I lived with my mother), but Maman told me that he made his without any liquid, just butter, eggs, and flour. I guess I inherited some baker's DNA from him, because I use very little water in mine. I also use much less butter, even though when I was with Mr. Lenôtre, our brioche dough was loaded with it. The dough is very rich and airy and soft, and is ready to absorb any flavors you can possibly want to add to it.

Note: Because the finished brioche needs airiness, use a high-gluten flour, which stretches to create little air pockets in the dough as it rises.

        ✳ MAKES 2½ POUNDS DOUGH

3 cups high-gluten bread flour

¼ cup sugar

1 package (or 2¼ teaspoons) active
    dry yeast

1 pinch salt

4 eggs

½ cup plus 2 tablespoons warm water

1 cup (2 sticks) unsalted butter,
    cut into small pieces and at room
    temperature

Place the flour in the center of the bowl of a stand mixer fitted with the paddle attachment. Pour the sugar, yeast, and salt in three different places at the edge where the flour meets the bowl. Break the eggs into a small bowl and place it near the mixer. Pour 2 tablespoons of the water directly on top of the yeast and start the mixer on low. Add the eggs to the mixer one at a time (they will "ploop" out of the bowl individually). When all the eggs are in, increase the speed slightly and slowly add the remaining warm water. When the water is incorporated, increase the speed to medium high and continue beating for 2 minutes. Turn off the mixer, scrape down the sides of the bowl, and beat for 2 minutes longer, until smooth.

Turn off the mixer and drop in all the butter. Start the mixer on low speed to incorporate the butter. Slowly increase the speed to medium, then high, stopping to scrape down the sides of the bowl after 2 minutes. Continue beating until the dough no longer sticks to the edges of the bowl.

Transfer the dough to a bowl large enough to allow it to double in size, cover it loosely with plastic wrap, and refrigerate it overnight. Use it within 3 days.

Belgian Glazed Brioche Tart

In my hometown, in fact all over the northeast of France and up into Belgium, a sugar-coated brioche was our version of a glazed doughnut. Now that Americans have taken up sipping cappuccino and café au lait (which Starbucks insists on calling a latte), I think you will find this very dipworthy. Hmm . . . brioche + doughnut. . . . Maybe this should be called a "bro-nut." ✳ SERVES 6

¼ recipe (10 ounces) Brioche Dough
    (page 8)
¼ cup sugar
1½ tablespoons unsalted butter,
    chilled

Preheat the oven to 400 degrees.

Place the brioche dough on a lightly floured surface and sprinkle some flour on top. Roll it out to make a 9-inch circle. Place the dough circle on a sheet pan lined with Silpat or parchment. Cover it loosely with a piece of plastic wrap and let it rise for 1 hour or until doubled.

Sprinkle the top of the dough with the sugar, leaving a ½-inch border around the perimeter. Cut 6 very thin slices of the cold butter and place them evenly on top of the sugar. Bake for 8 minutes, until golden brown. For an extra treat, serve with orange caramel sauce to dip your tart into.

✳

ORANGE CARAMEL SAUCE

1 orange
2 cups water
1/2 cup sugar
Juice of 1 lemon
(2 tablespoons)
2 cups orange juice
1 tablespoon cornstarch
2 tablespoons Grand
Marnier or other orange
liqueur or brandy

Zest the orange with a vegetable peeler or small knife, taking care to leave as much white pith on the orange as possible. Bring the water to a boil in a heavy medium saucepan. Add the orange zest. Simmer for 5 minutes. Transfer the zest and ⅓ cup of the cooking water to a blender (discard the remaining water). Pulse until the zest is minced.

(continued)

✳

Return the orange zest mixture to the saucepan. Add the sugar. Cook over low heat until the sugar dissolves, swirling the pan occasionally but not stirring. Increase the heat to medium and boil until the mixture caramelizes and turns a medium brown, 5 to 7 minutes. Test the color of the caramel by drizzling a spoonful of the mixture onto a white plate.

Standing back to avoid being splattered, carefully pour the lemon and orange juice into the pan. Bring this mixture to a simmer and stir until sugar crystals dissolve and the sauce is smooth. In a small bowl, mix the cornstarch with the Grand Marnier. Add this to the sauce and boil for 1 minute. Let the caramel cool and pour it through a fine-mesh strainer. Cover and refrigerate it until well chilled, 4 to 6 hours. This sauce can be prepared up to 2 days ahead. Remove it from the refrigerator 30 minutes to 1 hour before serving.

Cinnabun

Like me, this recipe is from the northeast of France, where it is called *bolux*. When I was an apprentice, day-old bolux was our everyday breakfast (and kindly Mr. Sauvage didn't even charge us!). My version is less complicated and time-consuming, since I make pastry cream in the microwave. The French version is made with rum, but I omit that and add cinnamon, which Americans love in their morning pastry buns.

* SERVES 8

FILLED PASTRY

1 cup milk

2 egg yolks

¼ cup packed brown sugar, dark

2 tablespoons cornstarch

½ teaspoon cinnamon

½ recipe (1 ¼ pounds) Brioche Dough
   (page 81)

4 tablespoons (½ stick) unsalted
   butter, softened at room temperature to texture of mayonnaise

½ cup raisins

½ cup apricot jam

ICING

½ cup powdered sugar

About 1 tablespoon milk

¼ teaspoon vanilla extract

Preheat the oven to 325 degrees.

Make the pastry cream by mixing the milk, egg yolks, brown sugar, cornstarch, and cinnamon with a wire whisk in a small microwave-safe bowl. Microwave on high for a total of 3 minutes, stopping the microwave after 2 minutes and whisking vigorously before cooking for the additional minute. Remove and whisk vigorously again. On a sheet pan lined with Silpat or parchment, spread the hot pastry cream in an even layer. Cut one or two large pieces of plastic wrap, place them directly on top of the cream to prevent a skin from forming, and wrap the entire pan. Refrigerate the pan for at least 30 minutes. (If you haven't already done so, this is a good time to prepare the brioche dough.)

Using all the softened butter, generously coat the inside of an 8-by-2-inch cake pan and place it in the refrigerator. Divide the brioche dough into a 10-ounce piece and a 6-ounce piece, and return the larger piece to the refrigerator. Roll the smaller piece of dough on a lightly floured surface into a 12-inch circle about ¼ inch thick. Place the dough circle inside the buttered pan and press it into the bottom and up along the sides. Refrigerate.

When the pastry cream has cooled completely, transfer it to a large bowl and whisk it vigorously. Spoon one third of the pastry cream into the prepared pastry bottom. Set aside.

Flour the work surface again and roll the large piece of brioche dough into an 8-by-12-inch rectangle about ¼ inch thick. Spoon the remaining pastry cream onto the rectangle so it covers the entire surface of the dough except for a 1-inch strip at a long edge. Dab a little water on this edge (this will allow you to seal the roll you are about to make). Sprinkle the raisins onto the pastry cream.

Starting from the long edge with pastry cream on it, roll the whole piece as if you were making a jellyroll, using the last inch of the dough to create a seal. With a sharp, serrated knife, cut the roll in half, then continue cutting the pieces in half until you have 8 equal pieces. Place the rolls, cut side up, in the pan on top of the pastry cream. Put a roll in the middle and arrange the others around it, leaving an equal amount of space between the rolls so they have room to rise as they bake. Bake for 30 minutes.

Let the pastry cool in the pan for 30 minutes. Warm the apricot jam in the microwave on high for 45 seconds (just until it becomes liquid), then remove the pastry from the pan and brush it with this glaze.

In a small bowl, whisk all the icing ingredients together until well combined. Add just enough milk to create an icing the consistency of maple syrup. With a spoon, drizzle the icing over the entire bun. Tear, cut, or otherwise separate the pastry into 8 buns.

Rum Apple Crepes

Stroll down any street, in any city in France, and you can smell the nutty, buttery fragrance of crepes cooking. French kids grow up eating crepes the way kids in America eat bread or kids in Mexico eat tortillas. In France we also make crepes every year on February 2, which is Chandeleur (or Candlemas). It's interesting to me that both the Christian and the Jewish traditions have a festival of lights and that both faiths mark the occasion with a pancake feast. The Christian one is celebrated with crepes and the Jewish one with potato pancakes, often served, as these are, with applesauce. Tradition states that if you catch a crepe with a frying pan after tossing it in the air with your left hand while holding a gold coin in your right hand, you will become rich. (I am right-handed, alas!)

The filling is Americanized here, using both rum-laced apples and homemade applesauce.

If you are an extreme dessert lover, pipe some Cinnamon Crème Anglaise (page 163) on top of the crepes and then add in the whipped cream as described below.   ✳ SERVES 8

CREPES
1 cup all-purpose flour
1 tablespoon granulated sugar
1 pinch salt
1⅓ cups milk, at room temperature
2 eggs, at room temperature
1 teaspoon vanilla extract

APPLE FILLING AND APPLESAUCE
4 tablespoons (½ stick) unsalted
   butter
10 large Fuji apples, peeled,

quartered, cored, and cut into
⅜-inch-thick slices
½ cup packed brown sugar, dark
½ teaspoon salt
3 tablespoons dark rum
1¼ cups unsweetened hard or soft
apple cider or unsweetened apple
juice, plus more if needed

FINISHING

3 tablespoons unsalted butter, melted
2 tablespoons packed brown sugar,
dark
½ cup heavy cream
1 tablespoon granulated sugar

For the crepes, mix together the flour, sugar, and salt in a
large bowl. Add all the milk at once and whisk with a wire whisk
quickly so no lumps will form. Add the eggs and vanilla and
whisk until smooth. Refrigerate the batter for at least 1 hour.

Place an 8-inch crepe pan or a nonstick skillet over medium-
high heat. When it is hot, remove it from the heat and spray it
with nonstick butter spray or use plain butter. Measure about 3
tablespoons of batter into a small ladle and use that as your
measurement for making each crepe. Ladle the batter into the
edge of the pan. Quickly tilt and rotate the pan until the bottom
is covered with a thin layer of batter.

Return the crepe pan to the heat. Cook for about 1 minute,
or until the bottom is light brown. Release the crepe from the
pan with a small metal offset spatula and flip it. Cook until the
second side is brown, about 30 seconds. Slide it out onto a

plate. Repeat with the remaining batter, stacking the finished crepes and separating them with pieces of parchment paper if you are not going to use them the same day. (The crepes can be prepared ahead, cooled, covered, and set aside at room temperature for several hours, refrigerated for several days, or frozen for several months. Defrost frozen crepes in the refrigerator before continuing.) Stir the batter occasionally and spray the pan with butter after every couple of crepes, or as necessary.

Make the apple filling by melting the butter in a large nonstick skillet over medium heat. Add the apple slices, sprinkle them with brown sugar and salt, and cook, stirring frequently, until they are tender when pierced with a knife, about 15 minutes. Increase the heat for the last couple of minutes to evaporate any liquid. Pour the rum into the edge of the pan, heat briefly, and carefully ignite it with a long match. Stir to distribute the flame. The rum will burn for about 30 seconds. Set aside half of the cooked apples for filling.

To make the applesauce, transfer the remaining half of the cooked apples to a blender and add the cider. Blend until completely smooth. Add more cider as necessary to create a saucelike consistency. (The applesauce can be prepared ahead and set aside at room temperature for 1 hour or refrigerated. Remove it from the refrigerator several hours ahead and serve at room temperature.)

To assemble the crepes, butter a large baking dish at least 11 by 15 inches. Using about ⅓ cup apple slices, form a log down one side of a crepe, ½ inch in from the bottom edge. Fold the bottom edge over the apples and roll it like a jellyroll, folding in the sides. As you fill the crepes, place them, seam side down, in a single layer in the prepared dish. (At this point, the crepes can be covered with plastic wrap and set aside at room temperature for several hours or refrigerated overnight. Bring them to room temperature before baking.)

To serve, preheat the oven to 425 degrees. Brush the crepes with the melted butter and sprinkle with brown sugar. Cover the dish with aluminum foil and bake until heated through, 5 to 7 minutes. Turn the oven up to broil, uncover the dish, and brown the crepes slightly, watching carefully so they don't burn. Whip the cream in the bowl of a stand mixer fitted with the whisk attachment, adding the granulated sugar little by little until firm. Spoon the whipped cream into a pastry bag fitted with a ½-inch tip.

Ladle applesauce into the center of the plates, tilting the plate so the sauce spreads evenly. Transfer 2 crepes, seam side down, to each plate using a large spatula.

Pipe decorative dots of whipped cream in a circle around the crepes. Drag a knife tip through each circle, forming a tail that connects each circle with the next.

Cherry Clafouti

I am always excited when cherries usher in the summer. All those beautiful blossoms of spring become mountains of cherries. In France this is the signal for home bakers everywhere to make clafouti, a very simple recipe but no less delicious because of that. (*Clafouti* is right up there with *frangipane* among fun-to-say dessert words. It seems like a name for a circus performer—Cherry Clafouti and his Amazing Acrobats.) Traditionally, we make it with whole, unpitted cherries. Just like cooking meat on the bone, cooking cherries with their pits lends a magical flavor and texture boost, even if it is a bit more work on your plate. My recipe calls for a batter that is less cakey and more crepelike or custardy than many others. I like the slithery sweet creaminess that swaddles the smooth, round cherries. You should experiment on your own with other fruits and fillings. Because the batter is so simple, the success of this dessert really relies on the flavor of the fruit. If you cannot find good cherries, try using whatever other fruits are in season and perfectly ripe: plums, peaches, apricots, blueberries, or blackberries. No matter what you do, it is hard to mess up. I have made this batter with half apple juice and half nonfat milk. I have added vanilla, cinnamon, chopped almonds, so please experiment.

* SERVES 6 TO 8

CLAFOUTI

1 cup all-purpose flour

½ teaspoon salt

1 cup sugar

2 cups milk

3 eggs

4 cups cherries (1 pound),
   destemmed, washed, and dried

1 cup heavy cream
2 tablespoons sugar

Start the batter by placing the flour, salt, and sugar in a large bowl. Stir them with a whisk to incorporate the ingredients and break up any lumps that might be in the flour. Pour the milk into the dry ingredients at once with one hand while whisking quickly with the other hand to avoid lumps. If a few remain, strain the batter. In a separate bowl, whisk the eggs and then beat them into the batter until smooth. Let the batter rest in the refrigerator for 2 hours.

Near the end of the chilling time, preheat the oven to 325 degrees and position a rack in the middle.

Place the cherries in the bottom of a 10-inch round glass or ceramic pie plate. Choose a dish that looks nice, as this will be the serving dish. Pour the batter over the cherries and bake for 1 hour, until the edges are set but the center is still slightly jiggly.

Meanwhile, whip the cream in the bowl of a stand mixer fitted with the whisk attachment, adding the sugar little by little until firm. Transfer to a clean bowl and refrigerate.

Spoon the clafouti into dishes while still warm and serve with a dollop of whipped cream.

Charlotte Nora

The story goes that the immortal chef Carême invented this cake and named it after Charlotte, the wife of mad King George III. I am not so sure that the greatest French chef of his time named a cake after another country's queen. I have also read that *charlotte* is a French version of the old English word *charlyt*, which means a dish with custard filling. While the professors sort this out, I offer you this recipe. Basically it is a crown of ladyfingers given extra structure with xanthan gum, soaked in a gelatin syrup with brown sugar, milk, and vanilla, then filled with chocolate mousse. I think the heftier taste of brown sugar in the soaking syrup helps unite the flavors of the ladyfingers with the chocolate. There are a lot of steps to this recipe, but you can do much of the work in advance and freeze or refrigerate. When Wendy Ripley and Jack Revelle tested this recipe for us, their sous-chef was young Nora Ripley-Grant. She is eight years old, and the finished result came out *magnifique*. If she can do it, you can do it.

Note: This recipe makes about twenty ladyfingers, as well as the 6-inch disk that serves as a base for the cake. To prepare in advance, when the ladyfingers are baked, simply wrap the sheet pan well with plastic or store them in an airtight container. They will keep nicely in the freezer for up to two weeks.

❋ SERVES 8 TO 10

LADYFINGERS

5 eggs, separated
½ cup sugar
1 teaspoon warm water
½ teaspoon xanthan gum
1¼ cups pastry flour, sifted
½ cup powdered sugar for dusting

1 cup whole milk

2 teaspoons unflavored gelatin

¼ cup granulated sugar

2 vanilla beans, cut lengthwise,
    or 2 teaspoons vanilla extract

2 egg yolks

1 cup low-fat milk

½ cup packed light brown sugar

1 cup heavy cream

CHOCOLATE MOUSSE

5 ounces semisweet chocolate,
    cut in small pieces

1 tablespoon water

4 whole eggs, separated

¼ cup plus 1 tablespoon granulated
    sugar

6 tablespoons unsalted butter,
    at room temperature

FINISHING

1 large bar dark chocolate, placed
    in the freezer until very cold,
    for making curls

Powdered sugar for dusting

Preheat the oven to 350 degrees.

Prepare a sheet pan for baking the ladyfingers by lining
it with a piece of parchment paper. Using a pencil and ruler,
draw two pairs of lines lengthwise down the parchment to make
two 3½-inch-wide columns with 2 inches between them. Next,
create a grid by drawing perpendicular lines every 2 inches.

You should be able to make eight lines. Flip the parchment paper over so you can see the lines but your ladyfingers won't come into contact with the lead from the pencil. On a second sheet of parchment, placed on a second sheet pan, draw lines for five more ladyfingers and a 6-inch circle as a pattern for the base of the charlotte. Turn this parchment over as well.

Begin making the ladyfingers by placing the egg yolks with half of the sugar and the warm water in a stand mixer fitted with a wire whisk attachment. Whip for 5 minutes on high, until thick and pale yellow. Transfer the mixture to a small bowl, and wash and dry the mixer bowl and whisk. Place the egg whites in the bowl and whip on high for 1 minute. Turn off the mixer and add the xanthan gum. Turn on full speed and add the rest of the sugar, 1 tablespoon at a time, until the egg whites are firm and glossy, about 5 minutes. Remove the bowl from the stand and pour the egg yolks and flour on top of the egg whites. Fold with a rubber spatula until well blended.

Attach a ⅝-inch tip to a pastry bag and fill the bag with the batter. Pipe the ladyfingers, following the guidelines you drew on the parchment paper. You should be able to make 16 on the first sheet pan. On the second sheet pan, begin to fill in the circle pattern, starting from the center. Pipe in a spiral, circular pattern. Pipe the 5 remaining ladyfingers last.

Dust the ladyfingers with powdered sugar by placing the sugar in a strainer and tapping its side as you hold it over the ladyfingers. Wait a couple of minutes and dust the ladyfingers a second time. The circular base does not need powdered sugar, but don't worry if you get some on it. Bake for 12 minutes.

While the ladyfingers bake, begin preparing the cream filling. In a medium saucepan, bring the whole milk to a boil. Put 1 teaspoon of the gelatin in a small bowl and add half of the hot milk to melt the gelatin. Stir the gelatin until dissolved and set it aside for a few minutes. Add the gelatin mixture, sugar, and either 1 teaspoon of vanilla extract or the seeds scraped from one split vanilla bean to the hot milk in the pan and bring it back to a boil, stirring occasionally with a wire whisk.

In a medium bowl, stir the egg yolks together and add 1 tablespoon of the hot milk, whisking to gently warm the yolks. Whisk a couple more spoonfuls of hot milk into the yolks and then add the rest of the milk, whisking constantly. Pour the hot mixture through a fine-mesh strainer. Pour and spread the filling onto a sheet pan lined with Silpat or parchment paper and cover it with plastic wrap, allowing the plastic to touch the cream to avoid forming a skin. Let the filling cool on the counter.

Meanwhile, start building the charlotte.

In a small saucepan, make the soaking syrup by whisking together the nonfat milk, 1 teaspoon vanilla extract (or seeds scraped from one split vanilla bean), the brown sugar, and the remaining teaspoon gelatin. Bring the syrup to a boil, then immediately transfer it to a bowl wide enough to allow you to dip the ladyfingers. Cool to room temperature.

Line a sheet pan with parchment paper and place a 9-inch cake ring on it. Place a second sheet pan nearby. Cut one end of each ladyfinger so they are all the same length and flat on one end. When the syrup is cool, dip each ladyfinger, top side down, for about 4 seconds, in the syrup. Place it undipped side down on the unlined pan so the syrup can soak in.

Place the circular cake base inside the ring. Line the inside of the ring with the ladyfingers, placing the flat ends against the cake base and standing them straight up with their pretty, crunchy sides facing outward. They should fit tightly. If there are gaps between the disk and the ladyfingers, fill them with pieces of leftover ladyfingers.

When the filling has cooled completely, transfer it to the bowl of a stand mixer fitted with the paddle attachment and mix it on high to a creamy consistency. Lightly whip the heavy cream. Fold the whipped cream into the pastry cream with a rubber spatula until well blended. Pour the filling into the center of the ladyfinger crown and put it in the freezer while you make the chocolate mousse.

For the mousse, place the chocolate in a medium microwave-safe bowl. Microwave on high at 30-second intervals, stirring in between, until melted. Allow the bowl to sit at room temperature until the chocolate cools to body temperature. Test this by dabbing a small amount on your lower lip; it should not feel hot, but rather slightly warm.

Meanwhile, whisk together the water, egg yolks, and 1 tablespoon of the sugar in a medium heatproof bowl. Place the bowl over a large pan of simmering water and whisk constantly for about 5 minutes, or until the mixture has thickened and is a creamy light yellow. Remove it from the heat. The yolk mixture should be warm to the touch.

When both the chocolate and the yolk mixtures are at the correct temperature, stir the yolk mixture into the chocolate.

Using a rubber spatula, stir in half of the butter until incorporated, then add the remaining butter. If it does not melt completely, place the bowl over the simmering water briefly, just to finish melting the butter.

Place the egg whites in the bowl of a stand mixer fitted with the whisk attachment and beat on high for about 1 minute, until the whites are foamy. Add the remaining ¼ cup sugar 1 tablespoon at a time and beat just until stiff, glossy peaks form; do not overbeat. Gently stir a third of the egg whites into the chocolate mixture. Then carefully fold in the remaining whites with a rubber spatula. Do not overwork; you do not want the whites to separate.

Pour the chocolate mousse on top of the charlotte. Transfer it to a serving platter and refrigerate it until ready to serve.

Shortly before serving, make the chocolate curls. Using a vegetable peeler, scrape curls from the edge of the chilled chocolate bar. Sprinkle the curls on top of the chocolate mousse and finish with a dusting of powdered sugar.

Chocolate Éclairs

How much do I love éclairs? Let me tell you a story. When I was eight years old, I began to go into the countryside with my brothers and sisters to gather wild daffodils. We would divide them into little bunches tied with string and then sell them on the streets of our town. The people were so nice and, perhaps remembering their own childhoods, would smile and buy our pretty flowers. I could spend the pocket money on anything I liked. Did I get new shoes (which I needed)? Or a comic book (which I didn't need but liked)? No—all of my flower funds went to buy éclairs.

Since I was so crazy about the éclairs Madame Germain sold in her bakeshop, I figured that the pastries she placed next to them in her showcase—which were three times as expensive as her beloved éclairs—must be even better, so one day I bought one.

Madame Germain wrapped it carefully and I left her shop as proud as someone who had just bought a new car and was very eager to try it. I unwrapped the package, full of anticipation, and bit into the object of my affection, closing my eyes so that I could fully savor the taste. "Pork? Salt? Liver?" I remember asking myself in disbelief. In fact it was all of the above. The super-expensive pastry that I had assumed would transport me to new levels of dessert pleasure turned out to be a meat pie!

Nevertheless, my love for éclairs was in no way diminished. I still believe they are a perfect treat. Crisp, light pastry; silky smooth icing; cool, sweet, and creamy on the inside. They are like dessert hot dogs.

In America, as in France, home chefs rarely make éclairs. "Oh, you can buy them at the store," people say. But, as you will see, they are not terribly difficult, and with my quick dough, it is much less complicated than the classic recipe. You'll also notice that I use the microwave to make the pastry cream much more quickly than you can do it on the stovetop—plus there is no danger of lumpiness. My chocolate icing gains richness and complexity with the addition of apple jelly. It's another layer of flavor. The tart fruitiness of the apple keeps the chocolate in the icing from overwhelming your palate, and the apple's natural thickening ability (because it contains pectin) helps firm the icing.

A final word: If you have always thought éclairs must be made at the last minute so the pastry stays crispy, that's another worry to cross off your list. When I was an apprentice in France, we used to fill our éclairs at six in the morning. By the time the customers bought them, hours later, the outside was still crispy, and the inside crust, where it came up into contact with the filling, had developed a wonderful soft skin.

* SERVES 8 (OR 4 GLUTTONS)

FILLED ÉCLAIRS

1 cup whole milk

¼ cup sugar

2 tablespoons cornstarch

2 egg yolks

2 ounces semisweet chocolate, chopped

1 recipe Quicker Cream Puff Batter (page 104)

CHOCOLATE ICING

1 cup apple jelly

⅓ cup cocoa powder (Dutch process)

2 ounces semisweet chocolate, chopped

A few drops red food coloring (optional)

Preheat the oven to 350 degrees.

Prepare the pastry cream by whisking the milk, sugar, cornstarch, egg yolks, and chocolate together in a medium microwave-safe bowl. Microwave on high for 2 minutes, then whisk vigorously and scrape down the sides of the bowl. Repeat the microwaving for two more 2-minute intervals, whisking and scraping in between. Spread the hot pastry cream in an even layer onto a sheet pan lined with Silpat. Cut one or two large pieces of plastic wrap, place them directly on top of the cream to prevent a skin from forming, and wrap the pan. Refrigerate for about 1 hour.

Meanwhile, attach a ¾-inch tip to a pastry bag and fill it with the cream puff batter. Cut a piece of parchment paper the size of a sheet pan, then pipe a small dot of batter in each corner of the pan and place the parchment on top. Holding your pastry tip about ½ inch above the surface, pipe 4-inch bars 2 inches apart to fill the cookie sheet. You should be able to fit 8 éclairs on the sheet. Bake for 25 minutes.

Transfer the pastry cream to a large bowl and, using a wire whisk, mix it until smooth and creamy. Attach a ½-inch tip to a clean pastry bag and fill it with the pastry cream. Using a serrated knife, cut each éclair lengthwise three quarters of the way through so that it opens like a book. Fill each with a generous line of pastry cream and close it again.

To make the chocolate icing, choose a medium saucepan with a diameter slightly wider than each éclair is long. Whisk the apple jelly and bring it to a boil in the pan. Lower the heat and cook gently for about 10 minutes, until it is thick and glossy. Lower the heat again, to a simmer, stir in the cocoa powder and chocolate, and mix with a rubber spatula until well blended. If desired, you can cheat by adding a few drops of red food coloring for a darker chocolate color.

Line a baking sheet with parchment paper. Remove the pan of icing from the stove and, gently holding the bottom of an éclair in one hand (or with tongs), carefully dip the top in the chocolate. Place it on the prepared sheet to rest, and then dip the remaining éclairs. If you refrigerate the éclairs, allow them to sit at room temperature for about 1 hour before serving.

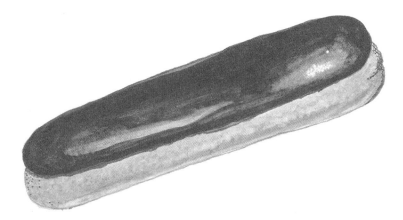

Quicker Cream Puff Batter
(*Pâte à Chou*)

Like many of the foods now associated with French cuisine, *pâte à chou* is said to have arrived with Marie de Médicis, who, according to legend, brought the gastronomically challenged French the recipes of Renaissance Italy when she married Henry IV in 1600. (If you believe all that is said about her influence on us, then before her arrival my ancestors must have been eating gruel and boiled turnips all day . . . every day.) This legend continues into the eighteenth century, when *pâte à chou* received its name from a pastry chef named Jean Avice, who called the cream puffs he made with this dough "little cabbages" (*choux* in French).

What do I think? It's probably no more complicated than the fact that cream puffs look like little cabbages, and sooner or later someone would have noticed. Come to think of it, they also look like Brussels sprouts, which are equally undessertlike.

But wherever it came from and whatever it is called, *pâte à chou* is nothing more than a simple mixture of flour, eggs, butter, and liquid—a variation on a basic white sauce. The traditional recipe calls for water, but, as elsewhere in dessert making, I don't see the point in adding something tasteless, such as water, when you can find another ingredient, in this case milk, that works just as well but also adds flavor and richness.

Also, the classic recipe calls for more steps and longer cooking of the batter. Trust me, for thirty years I have been making my batter much more quickly with fewer steps, and it always works. Tradition says you add your eggs one at a time and mix. I put mine in all at once. I have found that the extra mixing called for in the standard recipe book can lead to overmixing, which "wakes up" the glutens, resulting in cracking in the oven. For the same reason, I use a whisk rather than the wooden spatula normally used. The texture must be smooth, like a baby's skin. If it cracks, it won't be.

Finally, I lower the temperature. If you cook at 400 degrees, as many people do, the crust forms before the steam has expanded, and it will crack.

The bottom line is fewer steps, less mixing, lower temperature.

½ cup low-fat milk
4 tablespoons (½ stick) unsalted
   butter, cut into small pieces
1 pinch salt
1 pinch sugar
½ cup pastry flour, sifted
2 large eggs

In a small saucepan, combine the milk, butter, salt, and sugar over medium-high heat. When the butter is melted and the mixture reaches a boil, remove the pan from the heat and add the flour all at once. Mix with a wire whisk until the flour is incorporated, about 30 seconds. Transfer the batter to a metal bowl. Add the eggs, whisking well. At this point, the batter is ready to use in your recipe.

Chocolate Saint-Honoré Lulu

The original recipe for the Saint-Honoré cake is credited to a Parisian baker, Chiboust, who invented it in the 1840s and named it after the patron saint of bakers. I named my chocolaty variation after my father-in-law, Lucian, also known as Lulu. As a young man, he was capable of eating a whole one all by himself. I would like to see such a miracle. The trick for me in creating my version was not only to pick up on the chocolate theme, but also to make the finished dessert somewhat lighter, which I think I accomplished by using my cocoa whipped cream instead of the heavier Chiboust cream that is usually used. By the way, Peter Kaminsky's father is also named Lucian, so it is also in his honor.

* SERVES 8

CREAM PUFFS AND CAKE BASE

2 recipes Quicker Cream Puff Batter
   (page 104)
1 cup milk
¼ cup sugar
2 tablespoons cornstarch
2 egg yolks
2 ounces semisweet chocolate,
   chopped

CREAM PUFF GLAZE AND FINISHING

6 ounces semisweet chocolate,
   chopped
2 cups heavy cream
2 tablespoons cocoa powder
   (Dutch process)
¼ cup sugar

Preheat the oven to 350 degrees.

Use one full recipe of cream puff batter for the cake base and the other for the puffs. Trace a 9-inch circle on a piece of parchment paper using pencil and a 9-inch dinner plate, bowl, or cake pan. Turn the parchment paper over and place it on a sheet pan. Transfer a full recipe's worth of the batter to a pastry bag fitted with a ½-inch tip and pipe a circle around the drawn line. Using about 6 tablespoons of the batter and spreading it thinly with an offset spatula, fill the inside of the circle with a layer about ¼ inch thick. The thin layer should touch the piped edge. Use the rest of the dough and pipe 16 to 18 little cream puffs approximately ¾ inch to 1 inch in diameter on the same parchment that surrounds the circle. Bake the cream puffs and the circle for 30 minutes, until golden brown. If the center of the circle rises, pierce it with a sharp knife to allow the steam to escape. Allow the puffs and circle to cool.

Prepare the pastry cream by whisking the milk, sugar, corn-starch, egg yolks, and chocolate together in a medium microwave-safe bowl. Microwave on high for 2 minutes three times, whisking well between cooking intervals. On a sheet pan lined with Silpat, spread the hot pastry cream in an even layer. Cut one or two large pieces of plastic wrap, place them directly on top of the cream to prevent a skin from forming, and wrap the pan. Refrigerate the pastry cream for about 30 minutes.

Transfer the cooled cream to a medium bowl and whip vigorously with a whisk until it is light and fluffy. Transfer the cream to a pastry bag fitted with an ⅛-inch tip. Make a small hole in the bottom of each puff with the pastry tip, and fill each puff with the cream. You will have pastry cream left over; set it aside.

The cream puffs are now ready to be glazed. Place the chocolate in a small bowl and microwave it on high at 30-second intervals, stirring in between, until melted. Sprinkle a few drops of water onto the bottom side of a sheet pan and cover it with a piece of plastic wrap. Dip the top half of each filled cream puff into the melted chocolate and place it, chocolate side down, on the plastic wrap. Your fingers will get into the melted chocolate, but that's just one of the perks of dipping cream puffs!

Turn the 9-inch circle of pastry over and brush the bottom with the glaze. When it is set, place the chocolate side down on a serving plate. Pipe or spoon the remaining pastry cream into the middle of the round and spread it out, making sure you leave a clean 1-inch border around the perimeter.

In the bowl of a stand mixer fitted with a wire whisk, whip the cream, cocoa powder, and sugar until firm. Don't overwhip, or you will make butter! Fit a pastry bag with a ¾-inch star tip and fill it with the chocolate whipped cream. Pipe the cream, in any decorative pattern you like, into the middle of the cake. Cover all the pastry cream, leaving ½ inch of bare *pâte à chou* around the perimeter. To finish the cake, place the little cream puffs chocolate side up around the border of the circle, pushing each one into the whipped cream to form a crown. Chill until ready to serve.

Crème Brûlée Sandwich

This is an easy and quick version of a napoleon. I used to make it at Citrus in LA, and it was super-popular. Using phyllo layers interspersed with butter and crushed almonds is a delicious shortcut to the crunchy and sweet flakiness of more traditional—but time-consuming—*mille feuille* (puff pastry). And the flan is a lot less fuss than a heavier pastry cream. You can make the components in advance and assemble them à la minute. *See note on vanilla beans, page 27.*   ∗ SERVES 8

FLAN

½ cup whole milk
2 cups heavy cream
½ cup granulated sugar
1 teaspoon unflavored gelatin
2 vanilla beans, slit lengthwise, or
    2 teaspoons vanilla extract
9 egg yolks, blended with a fork

PHYLLO LAYERS

½ cup almonds
½ cup granulated sugar
8 sheets phyllo dough, defrosted in
    the refrigerator overnight if frozen
½ cup (1 stick) unsalted butter,
    melted
Powdered sugar for dusting

Preheat the oven to 300 degrees.

To prepare the flan, mix the milk, cream, sugar, and gelatin in a heavy, medium saucepan with a wire whisk. Scrape the seeds from the vanilla beans into the milk mixture and drop in the pods, or add the vanilla extract. Bring to a boil over medium-high heat. Remove the pan from the heat and let the vanilla beans steep for at least 1 hour, or until the mixture cools to room temperature. Remove and discard the pods.

Place a 9-by-13-inch baking dish in a larger baking pan. Pour enough water in the larger pan to come three-quarters of the way up the sides of the baking dish. Set aside the baking dish and place the water-filled pan in the oven to preheat for about 15 minutes.

Whisk the egg yolks into the cooled custard mixture and pour it through a fine-mesh strainer into the baking dish. Place the flan dish into the water bath and bake until the custard is set and a knife inserted into the center comes out clean, 45 minutes to 1 hour. Remove the baking dish from the water bath. Cool, cover, and refrigerate it until just before assembling the napoleons.

Increase the oven temperature to 325 degrees.

While the flan is cooling, roast the almonds for about 15 minutes, shaking the pan halfway through the roasting time. Cool the almonds, then pulse them along with the granulated sugar in a food processor until they are finely ground.

Reduce the oven temperature to 300 degrees. Line a sheet pan with parchment paper.

Remove the phyllo from its package and unroll it. Place 1 sheet on a flat work surface and cover the remaining phyllo with a slightly damp, clean towel. Brush the phyllo sheet with melted butter and sprinkle it lightly with the almond-sugar mixture. Top it with a second sheet of phyllo, pressing to seal.

Repeat the buttering and sprinkling process with the second and third layers, but leave the fourth sheet plain on top.

Using a ruler as a guide and a sharp knife, trim the edges of the phyllo stack to form a 12-by-16-inch rectangle. Cut the pastry into 3 strips lengthwise and 4 strips crosswise, to make twelve 4-inch squares. Transfer the squares to the prepared sheet pan in a single layer, using a large spatula. Place another sheet pan on top of the squares and bake until the pastry is lightly browned, 15 to 20 minutes. While the squares bake, repeat the process with the remaining 4 phyllo sheets and the remaining nut mixture to create 12 additional squares. Rewrap the remaining phyllo and refrigerate or freeze it for another use.

To serve, divide the flan among 16 of the pastry squares, spreading it evenly. A small metal offset spatula makes this job easier. To assemble each napoleon, stack 2 flan-covered squares then top them with a plain square. Place the napoleons onto dessert plates, dust them with powdered sugar, and serve immediately.

Triple-Chocolate Flourless Christmas Log

There are few invariables in food, but for a Frenchman, Christmas without a *bûche de Noël* is as unthinkable as a turkeyless American Thanksgiving. During the holiday season, we used to sell a thousand Christmas logs every year in Los Angeles—which is a lot for a bakery item—but at Lenôtre, we could sell as many as twenty thousand.

My version looks like the time-honored one, but instead of making a sponge cake roll, I make my cake with eggs, cocoa powder, and sugar. I know how tricky it is to make a cake roll and not have it break. That's why I bake mine for only four minutes in a hot oven, rather than drying it out for fifteen minutes in a low oven. You will also find that my mousse is lighter. And instead of a rum and sugar soaking syrup, I get more depth of flavor with brown sugar, dark rum, and orange juice. There's no way that they will be overwhelmed by chocolate.

I must take this occasion to share one of my favorite stories from my early career. François was the seven-year-old son of my boss Mr. Sauvage. It was Christmas Eve, and we worked all through the night, making hundreds of *bûches*. There was hardly any room to walk, so we started stacking them in piles that resembled a staircase. That morning, just after we had made the last *bûche de Noël*, François woke up early (don't all children wake up early on Christmas morning?). He saw the structure we had created and decided to run up the "stairs." He destroyed about thirty of our cakes before his parents stopped him. Poor petit François! The first thing he received that Christmas was a scolding.   * SERVES 10

5 eggs

⅓ cup granulated sugar

⅔ cup cocoa powder, sifted
(Dutch process)

SOAKING SYRUP

¼ cup orange juice

¼ cup dark rum

¼ cup packed brown sugar, dark

CHOCOLATE WHIPPED CREAM FILLING

8 ounces semisweet chocolate,
chopped

1½ cups heavy cream

CHOCOLATE ICING (GANACHE)

½ cup heavy cream

4 ounces semisweet chocolate,
chopped

Preheat the oven to 450 degrees.

Start by making the cake roll: Separate 4 of the eggs and place the yolks, along with the remaining whole egg, in a stand mixer fitted with a whisk attachment. Set the egg whites aside.

Add 2 tablespoons of the sugar to the mixer and beat on high for 5 minutes, until the mixture is creamy and light yellow. Transfer it to another bowl. Wash and dry the mixer bowl and whisk.

Place the reserved egg whites into the bowl of the stand mixer fitted with the whisk attachment and beat on high for about 1 minute, until the whites are foamy. Add the remaining sugar 1 tablespoon at a time until stiff peaks form. Add the cocoa powder and the egg yolks to the egg whites. Using a rubber spatula, fold everything together gently to keep the cocoa powder from puffing out of the bowl. Fold until all ingredients are well incorporated.

Line a 13-by-18-inch sheet pan with parchment paper and pour the cake batter onto it. Using an offset spatula, smooth out the batter, bringing it all the way to the edges of the pan. Bake for 4 minutes, until the cake springs back when touched and starts to separate from the sides of the pan. Immediately transfer the cake roll, parchment paper side down, onto a work space. Wet a clean kitchen towel, squeeze out the excess water, lay it on top of the cake, and let the cake cool.

Meanwhile, make the soaking syrup. Combine the orange juice, rum, and brown sugar in a small saucepan. Bring the mixture to a boil, stir, and remove it from the heat. Using a spoon, drizzle the syrup onto the surface of the cake; use all the syrup, making sure to soak the cake all the way to the edges.

To make the chocolate whipped cream, place the chocolate in a microwave-safe bowl. Microwave on high at 30-second intervals, stirring in between, until it is melted and warm (not hot) when you touch it. Set aside. In the bowl of a stand mixer fitted with the whisk attachment, whip the heavy cream just until soft peaks form. Using a rubber spatula, fold half of the whipped cream into the cooled, but not yet set, chocolate. When the ingredients are well blended, fold in the remainder of the cream.

Pour the filling onto the cake and use an offset spatula to spread it evenly. Bring it just to the edge of the cake, as it will spread slightly when it is rolled. Orient the filling-covered cake so that a long end is facing you, carefully separate about 1 inch of the cake from the parchment paper, and start rolling it into a log shape, gently peeling the parchment away from the cake as you go. When you have finished rolling, wrap the log snugly in the parchment paper. Refrigerate it until the filling is set, about 2 hours.

To make the icing, in a small saucepan, bring the cream to a boil. Remove it immediately from the heat and add the chocolate, stirring until it is completely melted. Allow the mixture to cool for 20 minutes, stirring occasionally as it thickens. This makes it easier to spread on the log.

To assemble the log, cut two long strips of parchment paper that are just a bit wider and longer than the log. Place these two strips, overlapping them slightly, on your serving dish (to keep it clean). Center the cold log on top of the parchment paper strips. Spoon the icing onto the log until it is completely covered. Using the tines of a fork, gently score the icing from the top to the bottom of the log, making lines to create the illusion of tree bark. Repeat until the log is covered with the tine marks. Once you are satisfied with the look, slip the pieces of parchment paper out from under the log.

If you do not need the cake right away, refrigerate it, but allow it to sit at room temperature for 1 hour before serving it.

Pineapple Rum Baba

If you have had *baba au rhum*, you probably know two things about it. First, it is made with a rich brioche dough; and second, it is soaked—I would say oversoaked—in rum. This version is less rich, but no less rich tasting; plus, it doesn't get you drunk. I know that sounds a little extreme, but I swear that there are bakers in this world who cover up the use of less-than-great ingredients and less-than-great technique with sugar and alcohol . . . lots of it. I tried to soak my baba with pure fruit juice, but I found that it would weep out of the cake. Adding gelatin was the solution. In my pastry shop in LA, we used to make strawberry baba and coffee baba. Here I use pineapple juice and rum, but you can use whatever you like.

Note: You can buy special baba molds—but you don't need them to make this recipe. Muffin tins work fine for individual babas, and any other cake pan will work for larger ones.   * MAKES 12 SMALL BABAS

BABA DOUGH
2¼ cups bread flour

2 tablespoons sugar

1 package (2¼ teaspoons) active dry
   yeast

1 pinch salt

½ cup warm water plus 1 tablespoon
   warm water

3 eggs, at room temperature

½ cup (1 stick) unsalted butter,
   melted

BABA SYRUP AND GLAZE
4¼ cups pineapple juice

2 cups sugar

2 teaspoons unflavored gelatin
Pineapple jam (or apricot, if you
    can't find pineapple), warmed
    to a syrupy consistency
2 tablespoons dark rum

WHIPPED CREAM
½ cup heavy cream
1 tablespoon sugar
½ teaspoon rum

To make the baba, add the flour to the center of the bowl of a stand mixer fitted with the paddle attachment. Next, place the sugar, yeast, and salt in three different parts along the side of the bowl so they don't touch. Wet the yeast with 1 tablespoon of the warm water. Start the mixer on low. In a small bowl, break each egg separately and add them one by one to the mixer bowl. Increase the speed with the addition of each egg. Finish by adding the remaining water little by little and increasing the speed to high. The dough should become elastic and pull away from the side of the bowl. Keep the mixer on high for 3 minutes. Then remove the bowl from the stand, cover it with a clean, wet towel, and let it proof in a warm part of your kitchen for 45 minutes.

Return the dough to the stand mixer fitted with the paddle attachment. Turn it on low speed and add the melted butter little by little. Increase the speed and mix until the dough comes away from the side of the bowl.

Place the baba molds or muffin tins on a sheet pan. Transfer the dough to a pastry bag fitted with a ½-inch tip. Fill each mold halfway, using a pair of scissors dipped in a small bowl of water to cut the sticky dough from the end of the pastry bag when you finish each one. Let the babas rise in a warm part of your kitchen until the dough reaches the top edge of the molds and forms small domes, about 30 minutes.

Preheat the oven to 350 degrees.

Bake the babas for 30 minutes, rotating the pan halfway through baking.

Meanwhile, make the soaking syrup. Whisk together the pineapple juice, sugar, and gelatin in a medium saucepan and bring to a boil. Cook until the sugar has dissolved. Let the syrup cool for 15 minutes. Place a wire rack on a sheet pan and set it nearby. Using a slotted spoon, immerse each baba in the syrup for 10 seconds. Transfer the cakes to the prepared rack. Brush them with the warmed jam.

When you are finished dipping the babas, strain the syrup and add the rum.

Whip the cream in the chilled bowl of a stand mixer fitted with the whisk attachment, adding the sugar and rum little by little, until firm.

To serve, place each baba in a shallow bowl and pour a few spoonfuls of syrup around the cake. Top each one with rum-infused whipped cream.

Praline Cake with Buttercream Mousse

When I was a young pastry chef in Paris, I made hundreds of these cakes for Gaston Lenôtre. He invented the classic recipe that is called a Succès (Success) in France. I don't think he would mind that I have made the recipe less sweet. When I first came to this country in the 1970s, chefs used twice the amount of sugar that we use in standard desserts now. I have also made the buttercream my own—it is lightened with egg whites and whipped cream. I strengthened my meringue with xanthan gum so it requires less sugar and adds up to a less heavy buttercream mousse. All that having been said, this is still very sweet.   ✳ SERVES 10

PRALINE POWDER

½ cup granulated sugar
Juice from ½ lemon (1 tablespoon)
1 ¼ cups sliced almonds

ALMOND MERINGUE

½ cup powdered sugar
1 ¼ cups almond flour (available at
    Asian or gourmet markets)
8 egg whites (1 cup)
½ teaspoon xanthan gum
½ cup granulated sugar

BUTTERCREAM AND FINISHING

2 egg whites
½ cup granulated sugar
2 teaspoons water
¾ cup (1 ½ sticks) unsalted butter,
    softened to the texture of mayon-
    naise

¾ cup heavy cream, whipped to
  form soft peaks
½ teaspoon vanilla extract
Powdered sugar for dusting

To make the praline powder, cook the sugar and lemon juice
in a small saucepan on medium-high heat, without stirring, until
the mixture comes to a boil and turns a light caramel color.
Add the almond slices, turn the heat to low, and stir with a
wooden spoon until the almonds turn a toasted brown color,
about 2 minutes. Pour the caramelized almonds onto a piece of
parchment paper, spread the mixture in a thin layer using an
offset spatula, and allow it to cool completely. Transfer the
cooled almonds to a food processor and pulse to form a coarse
powder. (Stored in an airtight container, this keeps for several
months.)

Preheat the oven to 275 degrees.

Make the almond meringue. In a medium bowl, mix the
powdered sugar and the almond flour together with a whisk. Set
aside. Place the egg whites and xanthan gum in the bowl of a
stand mixer fitted with the whisk attachment and beat on high
for about 1 minute, until the whites are foamy. Continue whipping and add 3 tablespoons of the granulated sugar. After 5
minutes, stop the mixer, add the remaining granulated sugar,
and whip on high for about 10 seconds. Using a rubber spatula,
fold in the almond flour mixture.

Trace a 10-inch circle on each of two pieces of parchment
paper and place them upside down on two sheet pans. Transfer
the meringue to a pastry bag fitted with a ¾-inch tip. Starting in
the center of each circle, pipe a pinwheel pattern to fill in the

circles. Bake for 1 hour and 30 minutes, then let the meringues cool completely.

Stack the meringues and, using a serrated knife, cut off any edges necessary to make the rounds identical. Wrap them in plastic wrap and store them in a dry area of your kitchen. (The meringue can be stored this way for several days.)

When you are ready to make the cake, start by cutting a circle of cardboard measuring 10 ¼ inches in diameter. Brush a little bit of jam (any flavor) on the cardboard to keep the meringue from slipping. Place a meringue on top of the cardboard, centering it carefully.

Make the buttercream by placing the egg whites and ½ teaspoon of the sugar in the bowl of a stand mixer fitted with the whisk attachment. Pour the remaining sugar and the water into a small saucepan and stir to mix. Start beating the egg whites in the mixer on high and at the same time start heating the sugar on medium. Bring the sugar to a boil. As soon as the sugar boils, reduce the speed of the stand mixer to medium and slowly drizzle the hot syrup into the egg whites, being careful to dribble it at the edge of the bowl to avoid splattering. Continue whipping until the egg whites are cool, about 5 minutes. Check the temperature of the egg whites by feeling the bottom of the mixer bowl.

Check the consistency of the butter. If it does not look like mayonnaise, place it in a microwave-safe bowl, heat it for a few seconds, and whisk to blend. Remove the bowl of egg whites from the mixer stand and fold in the butter, whipped cream, and vanilla with a rubber spatula. Set aside ½ cup of the filling. Use the rubber spatula to incorporate ½ cup praline powder into the buttercream remaining in the bowl. Pour this mixture on top of the prepared meringue round on the cardboard and use an offset spatula to spread it evenly out to the edges. Place the second meringue round on top. Refrigerate for 30 minutes.

After the filling has set, use an offset spatula and the reserved buttercream to fill in the gaps around the outer edge of the cake and create a clean finish. Pour the leftover praline powder into a large bowl. Holding the cake in one hand over the bowl, pick up some of the powder in the other hand. Press the powder into the sides of the cake so it sticks to the buttercream all around. Sprinkle the top of the cake with powdered sugar.

Refrigerate the dessert until 1 hour before you are ready to serve it. Cut it carefully with a large, serrated knife.

Galette des Rois (Kings' Cake)

Puff pastry can be used in so many ways. Granted, it takes time to make, but once it is done you can freeze it in batches and turn out amazingly impressive desserts, such as this one, in surprisingly little time.

Traditionally this dessert was served on the Twelfth Night of Christmas (January 6), but now people often make it as a weekend treat all through the month of January. Like many Frenchmen (and women), I have fond memories of the family gathered together for a Sunday meal. The youngest member of the family (that is, the youngest who can speak) gets under the table while one adult up above cuts the servings. The child under the table (sometimes more than one child goes under and they take turns) calls out the name of the person to whom the next piece goes as it is cut, so that they are randomly distributed. The reason for this is that the baker has often inserted a porcelain baby Jesus into the dough before putting it in the oven. As the galette bakes, the hole made by inserting it closes up and the location of the little porcelain baby is as well hidden as a truffle in the root-ball of an oak tree. Whoever ends up with the tiny Jesus is crowned the king or queen.

This galette is also known as a *pithiviers*, a word that English speakers find to be a bit of a tongue twister (try saying *pithiviers* five times and report back to me). A chef is not supposed to have one favorite dessert, but if this chef did, you might find that the buttery, nutty, creamy, crisp *galette des rois* does it for me.

* SERVES 8

½ cup (1 stick) unsalted butter, softened

1 cup almond flour (available at Asian or gourmet markets)

½ cup packed brown sugar, dark

2 eggs

¼ cup all-purpose flour

½ recipe (about 1 pound) Puff Pastry
   (page 50)

1 pinch salt

½ cup apple or apricot jam

Place the butter and almond flour in the bowl of a stand
mixer fitted with the whisk attachment and whip until creamy.
Turn off the machine and add the brown sugar. Turn the mixer
on low and gradually increase the speed to blend in the sugar.
Slow the mixer again, add one of the eggs, and beat until
creamy. Add the flour with the machine off, then mix just until
it is incorporated. Finish mixing in the flour by hand, using a
rubber spatula if needed. (Hand mixing is more thorough, as the
electric mixer does not reach the edges of the bowl very well.)
Cover the bowl of almond cream with plastic wrap, and leave it
out at room temperature.

Cut the puff pastry in half. On a lightly floured work surface,
roll each piece of dough into a circle ⅛ inch thick. If the dough
sticks to the rolling pin, sprinkle it lightly with flour. Using a
9-inch plate as a guide, cut out a 9-inch circle from each piece
of dough. Transfer each puff pastry circle to a parchment-lined
sheet pan. Refrigerate for 30 minutes.

Beat the remaining egg with the salt to make a wash. Scrape
the almond cream into the middle of one of the circles. Using an
offset spatula, spread the cream evenly, leaving a 1½-inch
border. With a pastry brush, brush the border with egg wash.
Place the remaining dough circle on top of the almond cream.

Press the two dough circles together at the edges to create a seal.

Brush the top of the galette with the rest of the egg wash. Using a sharp, pointed knife or a pastry tip, cut or punch a few holes in the top layer of dough to allow steam to escape as the pastry bakes. Refrigerate the galette for 3 hours to let the dough rest.

Preheat the oven to 325 degrees. Two hours before serving time, bake the pastry for 1 hour. Warm the jam in a small saucepan or in the microwave to make a glaze. When you remove the galette from the oven, brush it with the glaze to create a shiny finish.

Cool for 1 hour before serving.

Vacherin

Vacherin is nothing more than a traditional French slow-baked meringue filled with mousse, creams, fruits, or nuts. The meringue serves as a bowl for the filling, so instead of washing your serving vessel, you eat it. Mr. Lenôtre was famous for his mocha meringue, which I love, but I think the perfect partner can be found among the red fruits, especially strawberries. ✳ SERVES 8

MERINGUES

½ cup egg whites (from about 4 large eggs)
½ cup plus 2 tablespoons granulated sugar
½ teaspoon vanilla extract

FILLING AND DECORATION

1 cup heavy cream
2 tablespoons granulated sugar
½ teaspoon vanilla extract
1 quart vanilla ice cream
2 pints fresh strawberries, trimmed, or fresh raspberries
Red Berry Coulis (page 53)

For the meringues, line a sheet pan with Silpat or parchment. Position a rack in the center of the oven and preheat it to 200 degrees.

Place the egg whites in the bowl of a stand mixer fitted with the whisk attachment and whisk on high for about 1 minute, until the whites are foamy. Add the sugar

1 tablespoon at a time until the whites form stiff and glossy peaks. Add the vanilla and whisk until incorporated.

Transfer the meringue to a pastry bag fitted with a 1-inch tip or cut an opening directly in the end of a disposable pastry bag. Pipe 8 mounds, each approximately 2½ inches wide and 2 inches high, onto the prepared pan, leaving about 1 inch between each mound.

Bake for 2½ hours, rotating the tray once halfway through baking. At this point, the meringues should have a firm crust but will still be very delicate. If there is not a firm crust, return them to the oven and check them every 15 minutes until you can proceed.

Set the pan on a cooling rack and let the meringues rest for 5 minutes. Leave the oven on.

Once the meringues are firm, set out a small bowl of warm water. Turn a meringue over; the bottom will have a soft center. Using a spoon, carefully scrape out and discard the center of the dome, dipping the spoon in the water and wiping dry between scoops to clean it as necessary, until you have a bowl-shaped shell. Return the meringue to the baking sheet, scooped side down, and repeat with the remaining meringues.

Bake the shells for 8 hours, until they are completely dry to the touch. Turn off the heat and let the meringues cool completely in the oven. They can now be stored in an airtight container at room temperature for several days—or longer, depending on how well dried they are. The less moisture in the shells, the longer they will keep.

When you are ready to serve, in the chilled bowl of a stand

mixer fitted with a whisk attachment, whip the cream until soft peaks form. Add the sugar and vanilla little by little and continue to whisk until stiff peaks form. Transfer the cream to a pastry bag with a large star tip.

Pipe a round of whipped cream on each serving plate. Fill each meringue with ice cream and nestle it in the whipped cream. Arrange a circle of fresh berries on the top edge of each meringue. Drizzle about 1 tablespoon coulis around the whipped cream on each plate.

Saint-Tropez Tart with Raspberries

Saint-Tropez is a small port on the Mediterranean that became a chic vacation spot when it was frequented by Brigitte Bardot and many other French actors of the 1960s and 1970s. It also lent its name to the delicious pastry known as the Tropezienne. It looks like a huge hamburger bun made with brioche and filled with a mousselike vanilla cream. I have added my own twist, making it with raspberries. ✳ SERVES 6

PASTRY

½ pound Brioche Dough (page 81)

CARAMELIZED ALMONDS

1½ cups almonds, sliced

2 tablespoons granulated sugar

¼ cup water

4 tablespoons (½ stick) butter, melted

1 teaspoon vanilla extract

CREAM FILLING AND
TART ASSEMBLY

½ cup whole milk

2 tablespoons granulated sugar

1 tablespoon cornstarch

1 egg yolk

½ teaspoon vanilla extract

1 teaspoon unflavored gelatin

1 egg

1 pint fresh raspberries

1 cup heavy cream

Powdered sugar for dusting

Red Berry Coulis (page 53)

Flour your work surface and the top of the brioche dough and roll it out to an 8-inch circle. Transfer the dough to a sheet pan lined with parchment. Lay a clean kitchen towel on top and let it proof at room temperature for 2 hours.

To make the caramelized almonds, preheat the oven to 300 degrees. Place the almonds, sugar, water, butter, and vanilla in a bowl and toss to coat the nuts. Spread the mixture on a sheet pan and bake, tossing the almonds every 5 minutes, until they are golden brown, about 15 minutes. Cool the almonds completely in the pan, then place them in a jar with a tight-fitting lid and store them in a dry place. They will keep in the freezer for 2 weeks.

Prepare the filling: In a medium microwave-safe bowl, whisk together the milk, granulated sugar, cornstarch, egg yolk, vanilla, and gelatin. Microwave on high for 90 seconds, whisk again, and microwave for another 90 seconds. Cover the cream with a piece of plastic wrap placed directly on the cream to prevent a skin from forming. Set on the counter to cool.

Preheat the oven to 400 degrees.

To finish the tart, beat the egg to make a wash. Brush the brioche disk gently with the beaten egg, taking care not to deflate the dough. Chop the caramelized almonds to make 1 cup, and sprinkle the dough with the chopped caramelized almonds. Bake for 8 minutes, then slide the dough, still on the parchment, onto a counter to cool.

Use a large serrated knife to slice the cooled brioche in half horizontally like a hamburger bun. Place the bottom half on a serving plate.

Whip the cooled vanilla cream with a wire whisk until it is light and fluffy. Lightly whip the heavy cream until it forms soft peaks. Gently fold it into the vanilla cream with a rubber spatula. Pour filling into the center of the bottom brioche disk. Using a rubber spatula, spread the cream in an even layer, leaving about a ½-inch border. Take the biggest and most beautiful raspberries and arrange them around the perimeter of the brioche so that they touch each other and stick into the cream. You will need about 25 raspberries. Strew more raspberries all around and push them gently into the cream. Place the remaining brioche circle on top of the raspberries and cream, pressing gently so it adheres. Using a small strainer or sifter, dust the top of the tart with powdered sugar. Refrigerate until ready to serve. Drizzle the slices with berry coulis.

PART III

Made in the USA

Exploring a New World

America, for twenty-five-year-old Michel Richard, was truly a New World. It still is. What I love about this place is that everyone else is like me: we all came from someplace else—and brought our grandmothers' recipes. Meatballs and matzoh balls, frankfurters and falafel, couscous and cacciatore: We have the world's biggest collection of recipes handed down from endless sources. In the years I have been here, Japanese food and Thai food, not to mention the limitless varieties of Latin American cuisine, have all become mainstays of the American menu. Add to that the Mexican, Chinese, Italian, German, and eastern European cooking that came with the waves of immigration over the last hundred fifty years, and you have a United Nations of the world's food right here in the USA.

One of the big differences I found on arriving is that there are not as many pastry shops in this country as in France: most desserts are made at home. I have been very impressed with the quality of American homemade desserts. I shudder to think that when my mother made desserts at home and the recipe called for half a pound of butter, she would use a third of a pound of margarine instead. The result was a catastrophe.

Like every pastry chef I know, I spent years learning the classic doughs and crusts of French pastry. By the time I came to America, I thought I knew a lot. (Actually, I did know a lot, but there is a big difference between knowing a lot and thinking you know everything.) I appreciated this when I walked into a Kentucky Fried Chicken shortly after I moved to America. A thousand amazing little explosions crackled in my mouth as I bit through the perfectly crispy crust into a drumstick made by Monsieur le Colonel.

In France, we did not have such things. Our chicken never was crunchy in that way. Nor could I imagine any French army colonel, with a pencil mustache and stiff collar, opening a fried chicken chain. After biting through that crust and then experiencing the moist texture and steamy, chickeny aroma of that first mouthful, I wanted to meet this Colonel Sanders and invite him into the Legion of Honor. It made me appreciate the endless possibilities of crunchiness.

From that day to this, I have looked for ways to add crunch as the pièce de résistance to my dishes, whether they are appetizers, main courses, or desserts. I use many things to do this: almonds, pistachios, couscous, chocolate bits, crushed graham crackers. I am always on the lookout for more crunch helpers. Hence, I was the first gastronomic chef (to my knowledge) to make desserts using *kataifi* (a Middle Eastern shredded phyllo dough that gets super-crispy). I have found there are few recipes that are not improved by adding crunch. Crunch makes the food in your mouth dance.

America was, and still is, about big portions. I recall going into an Italian restaurant in Queens, New York, and ordering a plate of spaghetti. It was piled so high that you could not fit even one more strand on it. *This is truly the land of plenty*, I thought. It was the same with American desserts, as I soon found out. One of the items we offered at Lenôtre was a slice of layer cake that measured two by three inches. This was a nice size for a shop in France. We charged $3.50 for it (about $10 at today's prices). Meanwhile, the other bakeries in our neighborhood were selling much bigger pieces for much less. Their quality wasn't as high (and our competitors never claimed that it was), but I started to get the message that bigger is better in the USA. I remember going into a restaurant in LA in those early years and ordering a slice of chocolate cake—it was ten inches high!

"Who can eat such a big slice of cake?" I wondered. But I soon learned another American tradition: people share their desserts. And if there is any left over, then there is yet another American tradition: the doggie bag. This was different from my upbringing. When I was a child, I was taught to finish everything on my plate. This may explain why I have doubled my size since I came to this country.

Another dessert revelation was the cookie. You have so many of them. I was not raised in a cookie culture. True, we had our *madeleines*, *tuiles*, *sacristains*, and *macarons*, but not real *cookie* cookies like in America—the kind that cries out for a glass of milk alongside (an event I cannot imagine taking place anywhere between the Rhine and the Pyrenees). I remember the day I discovered the fabulous chocolate chip cookie, with its big chunks of chocolate and its crunchy nuts. Right next door to our *ooh-la-la* expensive French dessert store in Manhattan, there was a regular American doughnut shop. They had this strange—at least strange to me—chocolate chip cookie. It fascinated me. Soon I was deeply *amoureux*. Every morning when I got off the subway from my home in Queens, I bought one. I am not the only Frenchman to have fallen in love with *le chocolate chip*. All the famous French chefs who visit me—even Three-Star-Michelin gods—ask me for a chocolate chip cookie recipe.

America also introduced me to what I think of as "the caviar of sugars"—maple syrup. I had never tasted it before 1974. A woman friend took me to a New York coffee shop for breakfast, a classic place with red plastic booths and bright lighting, with a Greek guy behind the counter yelling orders to a Mexican fellow at the grill, where they serve Coke or Pepsi but never both, and where, in those days, the combination of cigarette smoke, steam from the home fries, and more steam from the coffee makers completely fogged up the windows. And the noise! The pans clattered, the dishes clanked, the air was filled with all the languages of the late-night people in their tuxedos (probably waiters), winding down their long evenings, and the early risers with their copies of the day's racing forms, considering the wagers they would place and the riches that would follow.

"Order the pancakes, Michel," my friend said. "You will like them." If I close my eyes, I can still see my virgin stack before me, golden brown, with a pat of butter melting on top and sweet stream rising from the deep amber syrup that covered it and dripped down the sides. The taste—my first—of maple syrup had the layers and slight nuttiness of the ultimate caramel. I was sold. For the next four years, I had pancakes with butter and maple syrup every Sunday. It was kind of my version of church.

In this section, I offer you recipes inspired by the desserts of my children's native land, the United States of America.

Macadamia Chocolate Chip Cookies

Go to any small town in the USA and pick up any church cookbook. What section has the most recipes? Cookies. Americans love their cookies so much that they even love a puppet with the fearsome name Cookie Monster. Out of all the hundreds of cookies—actually, out of all the thousands of American recipes I have read—if I had to pick one thing to eat that represents the delight I experienced in trying the foods of the United States, it would be the crispy, nutty, buttery, chocolate chip cookie. I have adapted a classic recipe and eliminated baking powder and baking soda (which I never use because I think they leave a bitter taste). Instead I let the eggs and butter do all the leavening work. Also, rather than relying on white sugar alone, I also use molasses to season the sweetness and deepen the flavor. I remember reading somewhere that macadamia nut trees were first brought to the United States as decorative greenery. I am glad someone figured out they are also good for eating, especially when they make my cookies crunch.

* MAKES 65 COOKIES

1½ cups (3 sticks) unsalted butter
1 cup sugar
½ cup molasses
2 eggs
1 teaspoon vanilla extract
3 cups pastry flour
1 pound semisweet chocolate chips
1½ cups macadamia nuts, toasted
   and chopped

Preheat the oven to 350.

Place the butter, sugar, and molasses in the bowl of a stand mixer fitted with the paddle attachment and beat until light and fluffy, about 5 minutes. Crack the eggs into a small bowl and stir in the vanilla. While mixer is on high, add the eggs to the butter mixture in two stages, stopping the mixer and scraping the sides of the bowl in between. Add the flour a third at a time, stopping the mixer and scraping the sides of the bowl after each addition. Add the chocolate chips and the macadamia nuts and mix until just combined. Chill the dough in the refrigerator until firm (about 30 minutes) to make forming the cookies easier. Using a small ice cream scoop or a tablespoon, scoop the dough into 1½-inch mounds with at least 2 inches of space between cookies. Bake for 8 to 10 minutes, or until light brown. The cookies should be firm around the edges but still soft in the middle. Allow them to cool on a sheet for 5 minutes, then transfer to a rack. Store in a tightly covered container for up to 3 days.

Extremely Chocolaty Chip Cookies

This cookie is not meant as an improvement but more as an *homage* to the chocolate chip cookie. I was also inspired by another American delicacy, the graham cracker—so simple yet so crisp and with such depth of flavor. I was struck by what a nice crust it made for cheesecake, so I started to play with it, chopping up hazelnuts and dark chocolate to go along with it. Because the graham cracker is already baked, there is no opportunity for gluten to develop to hold the cookie together, so it is naturally crumbly, even though the eggs, salt, and sugar serve to bind it somewhat. Take care to pack the dough very tightly as described below. The texture of these cookies makes me think of sand—not the grittiness of sand, but the way it is full of fine little grains. Try serving them with a scoop of vanilla ice cream on top—or use two spoons to shape the ice cream into oval "quenelles." ✳ MAKES 24 COOKIES

1 cup hazelnuts
14.4-ounce box graham crackers,
   crushed (about 4 cups)
8 ounces dark or semisweet
   chocolate
½ cup dark alkalized (Dutch process)
   cocoa powder
1½ cups (3 sticks) unsalted butter, at
   room temperature
1 cup packed brown sugar, dark
2 large eggs

Note: The cookie dough is rolled into a cylinder shape that can be refrigerated for several days or frozen for several months. Defrost it in the refrigerator before baking.

Preheat the oven to 325 degrees. Place the hazelnuts on a sheet pan and bake them for 15 minutes, shaking them once halfway through. Transfer the nuts to the center of a kitchen towel. Fold the corners of the towel over and let them steam for 1 minute. Holding the towel, vigorously rub the hazelnuts inside to remove the skins. Don't worry if a little bit of skin stays on. Cool the hazelnuts completely.

Place the hazelnuts and graham crackers in the bowl of a food processor fitted with the chopping blade and pulse to produce a fine powder. Roughly chop 4 ounces of the chocolate and add it to the food processor bowl, along with the cocoa powder. Process all together for 15 to 20 seconds, or until uniformly combined.

Using a spatula, mix the butter and brown sugar in a medium bowl. Add the eggs and the contents of the mixer bowl and incorporate well.

Divide the dough into halves. Lightly wet your work surface, cut a length of plastic wrap about 24 inches long, and lay it on the damp counter. Place one of the dough balls in the center of the plastic. Take one edge of the plastic wrap and fold it over the dough. Tuck it under and roll the dough, forming a large sausage shape approximately 3 inches in diameter and 6 inches long in the process. Roll up the entire length of the plastic wrap around the dough two or three times. Next, twist both ends of the plastic very, very tightly. If you loosely pack this dough, it will crumble too easily. Fasten the ends tightly with twine or twist ties. Repeat the above steps with the other piece of dough. Refrigerate at least 4 hours, or until firm.

To bake the cookies, preheat the oven to 325 degrees. Cut the remaining 4 ounces of chocolate into large "chips." Line two sheet pans with Silpat or parchment. Slice the dough into ½-inch-thick disks. Place 6 cookies on each sheet pan and press 6 to 8 chocolate pieces into the top of each. Bake the cookies for about 20 minutes. They will be very delicate—let them sit on the pan for 5 minutes until they are firm and cool enough to remove with a spatula. Carefully transfer the cookies to wire racks and cool completely. Store in an airtight container at room temperature.

Lemon Cheesecake Ice Cream

I love cheesecake. But sometimes a piece of this rich dessert feels too heavy, so I invented this frozen version. Same rich flavor, but lighter and refreshing. This may get the prize for Simplest Recipe in the Book.

Note: You won't need a fancy machine for this. If you don't own an ice cream maker, simply pour the mixture into ice cube trays and freeze. When you're ready to serve, place the cubes in a food processor and mix until creamy. You may need to refreeze and process the ice cream one more time for optimal smoothness.

✳ MAKES 1 PINT

1 cup whole milk
Juice of 1 lemon (2 tablespoons)
⅔ cup sugar
8 ounces (1 package) cream cheese,
    at room temperature, cut into
    ½-inch pieces

Place all the ingredients in a blender, hold the lid on tightly, and blend on high until very smooth, stopping a few times to scrape down the sides. The total blending time is about 4 minutes. Pour the mixture into another container and cover it. Refrigerate the mix for several hours. Process it in an ice cream machine according to the manufacturer's instructions (or follow the procedure for using ice cube trays described above). Transfer the ice cream to a covered container and freeze it for several hours before serving.

If the ice cream is frozen solid, soften it in the refrigerator or at room temperature until creamy, between 15 and 30 minutes. Serve in bowls and top with a generous drizzle of strawberry cassis sauce (page 35).

Almond Sugar Dough

My version of the French classic *pâte sucrée*. The desired result is a sweet, crisp crust. I find it much more flavorful to add almonds to the mix for depth and complexity. You should also note that I mix in only a third of the flour at a time. My reason is that don't want to wake up the glutens. I want to coax them to the point of awakening—but not send them jumping out of bed, because active glutens tend to make a tough dough. When I have mixed everything but the final addition of flour, I toss that in and barely mix it. If you do this correctly, you will have a crust with the pleasantly sweet, crunchy bite of a cookie.

Note: This dough can be made several days in advance and refrigerated, or it can be frozen for up to 2 weeks. Also, you can make a chocolate version by adding ½ cup cocoa powder to the dry ingredients.

✳ MAKES 1¼ POUNDS DOUGH

½ cup whole blanched almonds
½ cup powdered sugar
1 pinch salt
1 cup (2 sticks) unsalted butter,
   chopped into ½-inch cubes,
   at room temperature
2 eggs
2½ cups all-purpose flour

Place the almonds and sugar into the bowl of a food processor and pulse on and off until finely ground. Add the salt and butter and process until smooth. Add the eggs and a third of the flour and mix just until incorporated. Mix in the second portion of flour until incorporated. Add the remaining third of the flour in short pulses, just barely mixing it. Do not overmix.

Place the dough on a large sheet of plastic wrap. Flatten it out into a 1-inch-thick disk. Wrap and refrigerate for at least 3 hours before baking according to instructions in the recipes.

Corn Cookies with a Smidgen of Curry

In August, one of the most picturesque sights in the countryside around Washington is a fruit and vegetable stand. You'll often see one in the shade of a grand old oak or maple tree, displaying the summer's harvest in colorful stacks. If the stand is tended by a boy or girl of about twelve, with a big yellow dog wagging its tail and looking over the customers, then you have my sweet daydream image of America in summer: peaceful, pretty, and bountiful. Two words, on a big hand-lettered sign, always complete the picture: "Sweet Corn."

We don't use corn much in Europe—neither in desserts nor in savory courses. We feed it to the animals. Of course, the Italians have their polenta, which I played around with about twenty years ago—I came up with corn *tuiles*. But I never heard of such a thing as a full-blown leading player in a dessert recipe. The more I thought about it, the odder it seemed, because so much of the sweetness in candies and sodas comes from corn syrup. One day, I was walking up and down the aisles of Whole Foods and picked up a container of dehydrated corn kernels. They looked like little nuts, and it occurred to me that dehydrating them would naturally have concentrated the flavor and sweetness in the corn. I thought, *Why not use this corn instead of the almonds one finds in the traditional frangipane?*

You will probably wonder about one ingredient that I call for—curry powder. Trust me, this isn't a curry recipe, but curry, when used in very small amounts, has a way of waking up rich layers of flavor without calling attention to itself. I sometimes do this with shrimp as well. No doubt there are deep chemical reasons for this that the professors of Molecular Gastronomy could write books about, but all I know—and all that is important—is that it tastes good.   ✳ MAKES 20 COOKIES

½ pound Almond Sugar Dough
  (page 146)
1 egg, beaten
1 cup dehydrated corn
½ cup packed brown sugar, dark
½ cup (1 stick) unsalted butter,
  softened
2 tablespoons Wondra flour
1 pinch salt
½ teaspoon Madras curry powder
20 pecan halves for decorating

Preheat the oven to 325 degrees.

To prepare the pastry, roll out the dough to ⅛ inch thick. Cut out 20 circles with a 2¼-inch cookie cutter. Place the circles on a sheet pan lined with Silpat or parchment. The rounds can be close together as they will not change in size. Brush each one with a little beaten egg.

To make the corn frangipane, place the dehydrated corn in a food processor and pulse on high for 1 minute to create a powder—you should have about ½ cup. In a medium bowl, combine the brown sugar and butter. Stir in the corn powder, flour, salt, and curry until incorporated. Place 1 teaspoon of the corn mixture on each prepared pastry circle, leaving a ¼-inch border around the perimeter of each cookie. Gently press a pecan on top of each mound. Bake for 15 minutes, or until the edges of the cookies are golden brown. Let the cookies cool on the pan before moving them to a wire rack.

Haute-meal Cookies

Peter Kaminsky, who wrote a whole book about pigs, believes that there is nothing in the world that can't be improved with a little bacon. Recently, he came back from a visit with some fishermen and chefs in South Carolina. He told me about a wonderful chef named Jeremiah Bacon, who made ice cream with bacon. I thought Peter was joking—but he never jokes about bacon. "Michel, bacon has a sweet, salty, funky taste. A *grand chef* [which is how he always refers to me] could become a cookie immortal if he created a bacon cookie." I accepted his challenge, and in solving it, I believe I finally succeeded in my own long search for a new kind of oatmeal cookie. ✳ MAKES 24 COOKIES

1 stick plus 2 tablespoons unsalted
   butter, softened
½ cup packed brown sugar, dark
1 egg
¼ cup heavy cream
1 cup rolled oats
1 cup all-purpose flour
½ teaspoon vanilla extract
½ teaspoon cinnamon
4 strips bacon, cooked just until
   crisp, patted dry, and chopped into
   small pieces
½ cup pecans, roasted and coarsely
   chopped
Flaky sea salt (fleur de sel, optional)

Preheat the oven to 325 degrees.

Place the butter and brown sugar in the bowl of a stand mixer fitted with a paddle attachment and mix until creamy, about 5 minutes. Add the egg and cream and mix until well incorporated. Add the oats, flour, vanilla, cinnamon, bacon, and pecans and continue mixing just until blended. Wrap the dough in plastic and chill it for at least 1 hour (longer is fine too).

Line a baking sheet with Silpat or parchment. With a small scoop or spoon, form 1½-inch balls and place them in staggered rows on the sheet, as the cookies will spread when they bake. Top each cookie with a tiny pinch of flaky salt (or skip this step if you don't have any—they will still be delicious). Bake the cookies for 20 minutes, until slightly golden brown around the edges. Cool them for a few minutes in the pan before transferring them to a wire rack. Store the cookies in an airtight container for up to 3 days.

Baked Doughnuts

Here is an easy way to have hot doughnuts for breakfast in very little time, with no deep fryer or used cooking oil to deal with afterward.

Shortly after I opened my pastry shop in LA, a man came to me and said, "Michel, can you help me out? I want to open a doughnut shop, but I want to bake my doughnuts, not fry them." I was very busy at the time and couldn't help him.

Still, the idea stuck with me (don't get me wrong, I love a fresh doughnut in the morning, but like everyone else, I feel a little guilty when I eat fried things). Years later, I came up with this recipe. I used a light brioche dough because—well, to be perfectly truthful, I didn't know the recipe for doughnuts. I reasoned that if I baked them in a very hot oven, they would crisp up on the outside and stay moist inside.

I think of my baked doughnut as a negotiation with my food conscience. Since they are not fried, I feel I "deserve" my doughnuts. If you don't feel guilty about fat, feel free to make up the difference by filling the hole in the doughnut with whipped cream or ice cream. I won't tell.

> * MAKES 12 DOUGHNUTS AND
> 12 DOUGHNUT HOLES

1 recipe Brioche Dough (page 81)
1 cup sugar
½ teaspoon cinnamon

WHIPPED CREAM FILLING (OPTIONAL)
½ cup heavy cream
1 tablespoon sugar

On a lightly floured work surface, roll the brioche dough out ¾ inch thick. Line two sheet pans with Silpat or parchment and, using a 3¼-inch round cookie cutter, cut 12 circles out of the dough. Place these on one sheet pan about 1 inch apart. You should be able to fit all 12 on the tray. Using a 1½-inch circular cookie cutter, cut the center out of each circle. Transfer the "holes" to the other sheet pan, placing them about 1 inch apart. Cover the pans with a clean, dry dish towel. Leave the sheet pans out on the counter to proof for 1½ to 2 hours, until the doughnuts have doubled in size. Sprinkle each doughnut and doughnut hole with a mixture of cinnamon and sugar.

Half an hour before baking, preheat the oven to 450 degrees and position the rack in the center. Bake the doughnut holes for 8 minutes and the doughnuts for 10 minutes, turning the trays halfway through cooking.

If you wish to fill the doughnuts, whip the cream in the chilled bowl of a stand mixer fitted with the whisk attachment, adding the sugar little by little until firm. Transfer it to a clean bowl and refrigerate until you are ready to serve.

Almond Macadamia Brownies with Chocolate Nutella Glaze

I never ate brownies before I came to America. There was no such creature in France. I noticed them in the same shop on Fifty-ninth Street where I fell in love with doughnuts, which were also a novelty to me. While our customers at Lenôtre all wanted exquisite—and expensive—French *pâtisserie*, I was equally passionate about my morning doughnut and my afternoon brownie, both with a nice cup of American "java."

I don't claim to be able to improve on the hundreds of brownie recipes I have come across over the years, but I think you will like mine, which produces less fudgy brownies than many American ones. Also, instead of wheat flour, I use a mixture of almond flour and cocoa powder. For crunchiness you can't beat macadamia nuts. We made one test batch with salted macadamias, and they added a nice counterpoint to the richness of the chocolate—you may want to try it too. A final nutty addition is Nutella (a cocoa and hazelnut spread) mixed with chocolate in the frosting. Drizzle it on. It's very rich, so it doesn't have to coat the brownie in a uniform layer. ✳ MAKES 20 TO 25 BROWNIES

BROWNIES

6 ounces semisweet chocolate

1 ½ cups (3 sticks) unsalted butter,
   at room temperature

1 cup sugar

6 eggs, separated

¼ cup alkalized (Dutch process)
   cocoa powder

1½ cups almond flour (available at
   Asian or gourmet markets)

6 ounces macadamia nuts, coarsely
   chopped (salted nuts optional)

BROWNIE GLAZE
6 ounces semisweet chocolate
½ cup Nutella

Preheat the oven to 325 degrees. Lightly coat a 9-by-13-inch
baking pan with cooking spray and line it with parchment,
allowing a little of the paper to overhang on the edges.

To make the brownies, place the chocolate in a microwave-
safe bowl and microwave it at 30-second intervals, stirring in
between, until melted. Set aside.

In the bowl of a stand mixer fitted with the whisk attachment,
place the butter and half of the sugar and whip on high for 2
minutes.

Stop the machine, scrape down the sides, and push any
butter stuck in the whisk back into the bowl. Continue to whip,
adding the egg yolks one at a time. Turn off the mixer and scrape
down the sides, then, again whipping, add the cocoa powder and
melted chocolate. The total whipping time is about 6 minutes.

Transfer the mixture to a large bowl. Wash and dry the mixer
bowl and whisk attachment.

Put the egg whites in the clean, dried bowl of the stand
mixer fitted with the whisk attachment and beat on high for
about 1 minute, until the whites are foamy. Add the remaining
sugar 1 tablespoon at a time and continue whipping for 5
minutes, or until soft peaks are formed.

Fold in the almond flour to the chocolate mixture with a
rubber spatula. Add the egg whites on top and fold them gently
into the batter until blended.

Using an offset spatula, spread the brownie batter evenly into the pan and top with the macadamia nuts.

Bake for 30 minutes, then cool the brownies completely in the pan, at least 1 hour.

As the brownies cool, they will fall and will need trimming to create an even edge. Using the overhanging parchment liner, carefully lift the entire brownie out of the pan and place it on a cutting board. With a sharp knife, trim the edges to create an even rectangle with squared corners.

To make the glaze, place the chocolate in a microwave-safe bowl and microwave at 30-second intervals, stirring in between, until melted. Mix in the Nutella, blending well.

Drizzle the glaze—like the drippings on a Jackson Pollock painting—over the entire surface of the brownie. Place the brownie in the refrigerator for at least 1 hour to firm up. (It will keep this way for up to 5 days.)

An hour before cutting and serving the brownies, you can take them out of the refrigerator to allow the subtlety of flavors to bloom. However, if you serve them straight from the refrigerator, they are firmer, fudgier, more American-brownie-ish, and still completely luscious.

Maple Pudding with Strawberry Coulis and Lemon Milk Foam

Shortly after I began my first apprenticeship, my boss caught me off guard one day when he turned and asked me to get him some "chicken milk." First I pictured myself on a three-legged stool trying to milk a chicken. Then I just stood there, not knowing what in the world he was talking about, until he explained that chicken milk was a nickname for the egg-rich dairy product better known as custard.

There is nothing more creamy and smooth than custard. Ever since my kids were very small, I could always please them with a pudding made by throwing together some cornstarch, cream, eggs, and sugar in the microwave.

This dessert is based on that simple pudding as a foundation. The lemon foam and strawberry topping add tartness plus the sweetness of ripe fruit. I think you will find that this recipe is both delicious and interesting—it achieves a complexity through the use of different sweet ingredients: cane sugar (both brown and white), maple syrup, strawberries, orange juice, and good balsamic vinegar. If you can afford it, a bottle of thick, aged *aceto balsamico* (*molto* expensive) is the best ingredient I know of to wake up all the flavors in a perfect June strawberry.

* SERVES 4

MAPLE PUDDING

2 cups whole milk

4 large egg yolks

2 tablespoons cornstarch

½ cup maple syrup

8 ounces strawberries, washed,
   trimmed, and minced
¼ cup orange juice
¼ cup packed brown sugar, dark
1 tablespoon balsamic vinegar

LEMON MILK FOAM

1 cup whole milk
2 tablespoons granulated sugar
Juice of 1 lemon (2 tablespoons)
1½ teaspoons unflavored gelatin

GARNISH

4 beautiful whole strawberries

Make the pudding by combining the milk, egg yolks, cornstarch, and maple syrup in a microwave-safe bowl. Whisk until well combined. Microwave for 2 minutes on high, then whisk vigorously and microwave for 2 more minutes. Whisk and microwave the same way one more time and divide the pudding into serving glasses or small bowls. Let the pudding cool, cover it with plastic film placed directly on the surface to prevent a skin from forming, and refrigerate for a few hours, until cold.

Shortly before you are ready to serve, combine the ingredients for the strawberry topping in a medium bowl. Let this sit while you make the lemon foam.

For the foam, stir together the milk, sugar, and lemon juice in a medium metal bowl. Sprinkle the gelatin over the mixture and let it stand for 1 minute to soften. Set the bowl into a larger bowl of ice water and beat with a handheld electric mixer or an immersion blender at high speed until the mixture is foamy.

To serve, spoon the strawberry topping over the pudding. Add a dollop of the lemon milk foam. Garnish by making a slit in each whole strawberry and pushing it onto the edge of the glass.

Apple Fig Crumple

What's in a name? In the case of crumbles and cobblers, the very words sound fun and not very fussy. I picture an old shoemaker with a leather apron, pausing in his work, putting down his hammer, and taking a tea break with one of these simple desserts. I love the idea of them: sweet fruitiness and a crispy crumbly crust on top. I chose Fuji apples for this recipe because they retain their shape and texture rather than dissolving into mush. Then I tossed in some figs because, like apples, they contain a lot of pectin to naturally thicken the creamy compote that fills up the spaces between fruit slices. I threw a blanket of sweet almond meringue over the filling—it becomes infused with the sweet steam rising from the bubbling fruit. On the very top is a wonderful and delicate covering of crumpled-up pieces of phyllo. (When I was dreaming up this recipe, the idea of the phyllo in the almond meringue reminded me of young lettuces in a spring garden.) Finished off with a dusting of powdered sugar and sprinkled with almond slices, my crumple looks impressively fancy, but it is simple. I love it with a scoop of vanilla ice cream.

Note: If you can't find almond meal, make your own by finely grinding frozen almonds in a food processor until powdered. Freezing the nuts keeps you from having to add sugar; room-temperature almonds would turn into almond butter.

* SERVES 6 TO 8

FRUIT FILLING

6 Fuji apples, peeled, cored, and
   chopped into 1-inch pieces
4 tablespoons (½ stick) unsalted
   butter
½ cup packed brown sugar, light
½ teaspoon cinnamon
½ cup heavy cream

8 fresh figs, stems removed, cut
   into quarters

2 eggs, separated

¼ cup granulated sugar

2 ounces almond meal (see note)

3 sheets phyllo dough, defrosted in
   the refrigerator overnight if frozen

¼ cup almond slices

2 tablespoons powdered sugar

Preheat the oven to 350 degrees.

Spread the diced apples in the bottom of a large roasting pan
or glass baking dish. Cut the butter into small pieces and place
it on top. Sprinkle with the brown sugar and cinnamon. Toss the
apples and bake for 45 minutes, toss again halfway through the
baking time. Bake until the apples look caramelized and are
tender. Leave the oven on.

Transfer the filling to a 9-inch pie plate using tongs or a
slotted spoon so the juices remain in the baking dish. Pour the
heavy cream into the dish and stir, scraping the bottom to lift up
any remaining apple pieces. Return the dish to the oven for 5
minutes. When the cream comes to a boil, carefully stir and
scrape the bottom of the dish again.

Reduce the oven heat to 325 degrees.

Carefully transfer the liquid to a blender or food processor
along with 1 cup of the cooked apples. Holding the lid on tightly
to prevent the hot mixture from splattering, blend on high until
creamy. Pour this creamy applesauce over the baked apples in
the pie plate. Arrange the fig quarters evenly on top.

Start making the crust by placing the egg whites in the bowl of a stand mixer fitted with the whisk attachment and beating on high for about 1 minute, until the whites are foamy. Add the sugar 1 tablespoon at a time and continue whipping for about 5 minutes, until the egg whites are firm and glossy. While the egg whites are whipping, beat the egg yolks with a fork in a small bowl. Gently fold the egg yolks and almond meal into the egg whites, using a rubber spatula. Pour this mixture on top of the fruit, covering it evenly.

Lay the phyllo sheets, still stacked, on a clean work surface. Cut them in half lengthwise, and make three cuts vertically 4¼ inches apart. This will create 24 rectangles of phyllo. Pick up each piece of phyllo from the center of the rectangle as if you were picking up a handkerchief to put in a suit coat pocket. Then press the phyllo piece, point side down, lightly into the filling. Repeat with all the rectangles until the pie is covered with ruffled phyllo. Sprinkle with almond slices and powdered sugar and bake for 45 minutes, or until the top is lightly browned and puffy.

Let the crumple sit for 1 hour. Serve it warm or (for a thicker consistency) at room temperature.

World's Flakiest Apple Pie

I have always been told that lard makes the flakiest pie crust. I like flaky, but I don't like lard. I have debated this point with many friends. They took it as an article of faith that lard is the magic ingredient, but I bet them I could make a crust that is just as flaky using butter. In this recipe you have the result. By using a food processor to mix and coat little pieces of butter and then freezing them before proceeding, I get what is, in effect, free-form puff pastry. Instead of the orderly distribution of thick layers of butter trapped between equally thin layers of flour and water, this method creates hundreds, if not thousands, of randomly distributed little butter pockets in the dough. When you bake it, the butter melts, the water in the butter turns to steam, and that creates airiness, which makes for a crisp, flaky crust. Give yourself a head start. Making a perfect dough takes two days from start to finish (don't worry—most of it is "resting" time).

Note: You may want to serve this with vanilla ice cream and a dollop of Cinnamon Crème Anglaise (opposite). * SERVES 6 TO 8

WORLD'S FLAKIEST PIE CRUST

DAY 1
....

2 cups (4 sticks) unsalted butter,
    frozen and cut into ½-inch cubes
1 cup pastry flour

DAY 2
....

3 cups pastry flour
¼ cup granulated sugar
1 teaspoon salt
About ¾ cup ice water

CINNAMON CRÈME
ANGLAISE
(CINNAMON CUSTARD
SAUCE)
....

1 cup heavy cream
2 tablespoons sugar
2-inch piece cinnamon stick
2 egg yolks, lightly beaten
2 tablespoons dark rum

Combine the cream with the sugar in a small saucepan. Add the cinnamon stick, bring the mixture to a boil, remove the pan from the heat, and let it sit for 1 hour. Once the cinnamon-infused cream has cooled, slowly whisk the yolks into mixture. Add the rum. Return the pan to medium-low heat and cook, stirring, until the sauce has thickened enough to coat the back of a spoon. Pour the sauce through a fine-mesh strainer and discard

(continued)

*

the cinnamon stick. Cool it to
room temperature, then cover
and refrigerate it until chilled,
4 to 6 hours. Use the sauce
within 2 days as a topping for
such desserts as Mulled Cider
and Rum Risotto (page 41) or
the World's Flakiest Apple Pie
(page 163).

*

FILLING

12 Fuji apples, peeled, cored,
   and cut into quarters
1 cup packed brown sugar
¼ cup cornstarch
1 tablespoon cinnamon
1 teaspoon salt
¼ cup apple juice

FINISHING

1 egg, beaten with a fork
¼ cup sliced almonds
Powdered sugar for dusting

The day before you plan to serve the pie, put the frozen
butter cubes into a food processor and pulse them for 1 minute.
Add the flour and continue pulsing until tiny balls form. Transfer the mixture to a bowl, cover it with plastic wrap, and freeze
it overnight.

The next day, return the mixture to the food processor bowl.
Add the flour, sugar, and salt, and pulse, adding the ice water
1 tablespoon at a time, very slowly. When the mixture just starts
binding (you may not need all the water), turn the dough out onto
a lightly floured work surface and finish forming it into a ball by
hand. Wrap the dough in plastic and refrigerate for a few hours.

Preheat the oven to 325 degrees.

To make the filling, combine all the ingredients in a large
bowl, stirring until the apples are well coated. Pour the mixture
into a large glass or ceramic baking dish and bake for 45
minutes, stirring every 15 minutes. Let cool. Leave the oven on.

Meanwhile, prepare the pie shell by buttering a 9-inch pie plate. Unwrap the dough, cut it in half, then rewrap and return one piece to the refrigerator. Roll out the other half to form an 11-inch round ¼ inch thick. Gently wrap the rolled dough around the rolling pin, move the pie plate under the pin, and unroll the dough into the plate. Gently but firmly press the crust into place, and use a knife to cut the excess around the outer edge of the pie plate. Make sure you leave dough on top of the pie plate edge. Freeze the shell for 20 minutes.

Roll the remaining dough into another 11-inch round ¼ inch thick. Make sure it will fit over the top of the pie with a little excess hanging off the sides. Rewrap it and return it to the refrigerator to rest.

Line the inside of the pie shell with parchment paper. Fill it with dry beans or pie weights and bake it for 45 minutes. Remove the weights and parchment and allow the crust to cool on the counter.

Spoon the cooled apple filling into the par-baked piecrust. Brush the beaten egg along the edges of the crust. Lay the top crust over the apples and gently apply pressure to the edges to form a seal. Cut off any excess dough from the sides of the pie plate using a knife or scissors. Brush the remaining egg wash onto the top crust. With a knife or cookie cutter, make a ¼- to ½-inch hole in the center of the top crust. Sprinkle the sliced almonds on top of the piecrust and finish with a little powdered sugar.

Bake for 45 minutes, or until golden brown.

World's Flakiest Cherry Pie

Except for apple pie, it doesn't get more American than cherry pie. Let me rephrase that: It doesn't get more American than pie. We French make lots of tarts, mostly with no crust on top, but the art of putting a fruit filling between two flaky crusts—that is one of the essentially American things that I didn't know when I arrived but have since grown to love. So now that I have paid my respects to the red, white, and blue, I'll end this introduction by telling you of a German twist that I added to my cherry pie: bay leaves. The Germans often add bay to their cherry desserts. It is just the lightest, smoothest herbal infusion and creates an unusual but delicious flavor that eaters will notice but not quite be able to identify. Finally, I use cranberry juice in the filling because it introduces more fruity flavor without adding much sweetness.

* SERVES 6 TO 8

World's Flakiest Pie Crust (page 163)
2 pounds cherries, stemmed, washed,
    and pitted
1 cup sugar
¼ cup cornstarch
½ cup cranberry juice
2 bay leaves
1 egg, lightly beaten

The day before you intend to serve the pie, begin making the crust as instructed on page 164. The next day, continue with the process, par-baking the shell and allowing it to cool, then rolling out and chilling the dough round for the top of the pie.

While the par-baked pastry shell cools, place the cherries, sugar, cornstarch, cranberry juice, and bay leaves in a large saucepan. Bring the mixture to a gentle boil and immediately reduce the heat. Simmer for no more than 2 minutes—don't overcook, or you'll have cherry jam! Pour the cherry mixture onto a sheet pan and cool it to room temperature.

Preheat the oven to 325.

When the cherries are cooled, use a slotted spoon to ladle them into the piecrust, leaving the juice on the sheet pan. Reserve the juice.

Brush the beaten egg along the edges of the crust. Lay the top crust on top of the cherry filling and gently apply pressure to the edges to form a seal. Cut off any excess dough from the sides of the pie plate using a knife or a pair of scissors. Brush the remaining egg wash onto the top crust. With a knife or cookie cutter, make a ¼- to ½-inch hole in the center of the top crust. Bake for 45 minutes, or until golden brown.

Pour the cherry juice into a small saucepan and warm it over medium heat. Drizzle this sauce over each pie slice before serving.

Strawberry Chocolate Tart

The raw material of chocolate—the cacao bean—is almost as complex in its varieties and flavor components as the grape, the raw material of wine. The best chocolate in the world, from the highlands of Venezuela, has a distinct cherry note to its flavor profile. But the dessert maker or chocolatier doesn't have to stop there. He or she can expand on chocolate's fruit-friendly quality by actually adding fruit. For example, strawberries go particularly well with chocolate. Here, I incorporate strawberry puree into the chocolate ganache. The added body and moisture in the fruit allows me to cut down on cream and produce a deeply flavorful yet not overly heavy dessert. Try it with cherries or raspberries in season. Out of season, turn your thoughts to another dessert. Ideally, fruit should be eaten only in the season that Mother Nature intends.

½ recipe (½ pound) Cocoa Sugar
    Dough (page 169)
2 tablespoons unsalted butter,
    at room temperature
4 pounds fresh strawberries, washed
    and trimmed
½ cup sugar
7 ounces bittersweet chocolate
½ cup heavy cream
2 eggs

Preheat the oven to 325.

On a lightly floured work surface, roll the dough into a 12-inch round ¼ inch thick. With a fork, poke holes in the dough (this is also called "docking the dough"). Smear the room-temperature butter all inside a 9-inch pie plate. Carefully lay the dough into the pie plate and press it into place. Using a knife, trim the extra dough from the top edge. Place the shell in the freezer for 10 minutes. Cover it with a piece of parchment paper and fill it with dry beans or pie weights. Bake the tart shell for 20 minutes.

While the tart dough is in the oven, make the filling: Puree 2 pounds of the strawberries and the sugar in a blender until smooth and pour the mixture through a fine-mesh strainer. Microwave the chocolate on high, at 30-second intervals, stirring in between, until melted. Pour the strawberry puree into the chocolate and mix with a whisk. Stir in the heavy cream, whisking constantly. Crack the eggs into a small bowl and beat them together. Add the beaten eggs to the chocolate mixture and whisk until combined.

After the tart shell has baked, remove the weights and parchment and let it cool for a few minutes. Leave the oven on.

Pour the chocolate mixture into the shell and bake the tart for 30 minutes, or until the filling is set in the center but not solid. Test for doneness by shaking the pie plate gently. The tart should still jiggle slightly. Allow the tart to cool.

Finish the tart by arranging the remaining fresh strawberries, hull end down, around the perimeter of the tart.

COCOA SUGAR DOUGH

The only difference between this and my Almond Sugar Dough (page 146) is the addition of cocoa powder. Chocolate and almonds are natural partners, and there is very little in life that is not improved with a little chocolate. This dough can be made several days in advance and refrigerated, or it can be frozen for up to two weeks.

Makes 1 pound dough

1 ¼ cups all-purpose flour
¼ cup whole blanched almonds
¼ cup powdered sugar
¼ cup alkalized (Dutch process) cocoa powder
½ cup (1 stick) unsalted butter, at room temperature, cut into pieces
1 egg
1 pinch salt

Strawberry Cream Puffs with a Caramel Halo

I love the *idea* of strawberry shortcake, but I have to confess that I don't absolutely love the flavor because I find the baking powder used in the traditional shortcake a little bitter. Still, I won't try to win a fight with a fine American tradition; this is my variation on that theme. In France, we used to make cream puffs filled with pastry cream, and that gave me an idea. Why not cut a light, airy cream puff in half and sandwich it around whipped cream and strawberries? And to top it off, a crackling, sweet caramel hat that those who know traditional French pastry may recognize as the topper for the little cream puffs in the Christmas specialty *croquembouche*.   * SERVES 5 (2 CREAM PUFFS PER SERVING)

1 recipe Quicker Cream Puff Batter
   (page 104)

CARAMEL TOPPING
1 cup sugar
2 tablespoons light corn syrup

FILLINGS
1 quart basket strawberries, washed,
   stemmed, dried,* and cut into
   quarters
3 tablespoons sugar
1 cup heavy cream

....

*   Hint: Berries bruise easily if you try to dry them too vigorously. The way I dry mine is to rinse them and then place them on a dish towel or paper towel spread out on a sheet pan. Then, when I gently shake the tray, the berries roll around and dry on the cloth without the slightest damage.

Preheat the oven to 350 degrees.

Place the cream puff batter in a pastry bag fitted with a ¾-inch tip. On a Silpat- or parchment-lined sheet pan, pipe ten 2-inch mounds of the batter with about 2 inches space around each. Bake for 35 minutes, then set aside to cool on the pan.

Meanwhile, make the caramel topping. In a small saucepan, bring the sugar and corn syrup to a boil and continue cooking, without stirring, until the color changes to a light caramel. You can test the color by spooning a small amount onto a white plate—you are looking for a golden honey tone. Remove the pan from the heat.

Very carefully, holding the bottom of a puff, dip it in the caramel and place it, caramel-side down, on a sheet of parchment or Silpat. The caramel will set quickly, creating a beautifully golden and decorative top on each puff—like a saint's halo in an early Renaissance painting.

While the caramel sets, sprinkle the strawberries with 2 tablespoons of the sugar and let them rest for 30 minutes.

Just before serving, whip the cream in the chilled bowl of a stand mixer fitted with the whisk attachment, adding the remaining sugar little by little until firm.

To serve, cut off the caramelized top half of two cream puffs and set them aside carefully. Set the bottom halves of the puffs on an individual serving plate. Spoon the strawberries into each base along with some juice. Spoon a dollop of whipped cream on top of each mound of berries and replace the caramelized tops.

Quick Pecan Pie with Sorghum Molasses and Cranberry Curry Cream

When I first arrived in this country, I associated pecan pie with traveling. New Yorkers were satisfied with their cheesecakes and cannoli. Once you left "le Grand Apple," though, especially in the South, pecan pie reigned supreme. She was the queen of desserts, usually attended by her princely escort, a scoop of vanilla ice cream. One of the wonderful things about the traditional pecan pie made of cornstarch, Karo syrup, and pecans is its simplicity.

My version is quick and easy too, not so much a reinvention as a new piece of music based on an old melody. For starters, instead of a flour-based piecrust, I came up with a no-bake crust that features ground pecans, chocolate, and curry. Why curry? I love the way Indian and Pakistani chefs roast nuts seasoned with sugar, salt, and curry. Sorghum molasses is not really molasses: it is a sweet grass syrup made by the Amish in Kentucky. Nancy Newsom Mahaffey, who makes a wonderful American country ham, sent me some sorghum molasses and told me her father loved it on his biscuits. The sweet and spiced filling cooks quickly in the microwave—and the cranberry juice adds just enough fruity tartness to cut through the sweetness. The result is all about smooth texture with nutty crunchiness and great complexity of flavor that is bold instead of fussy.   ✳ SERVES 6 TO 8

NO-BAKE CRUST

3 cups pecans

2 tablespoons water

¼ cup sugar

½ teaspoon Madras curry powder

2 tablespoons unsalted butter

1 pinch salt

5 ounces milk chocolate

1 cup sorghum molasses

½ cup cranberry juice

½ cup heavy cream

½ teaspoon Madras curry powder

½ cup (1 stick) unsalted butter,
    cut into small pieces

¼ cup cornstarch

1 cup heavy cream

2 tablespoons granulated sugar

Preheat the oven to 325 degrees.

Start by making the piecrust: Sprinkle the inside of a 9-inch plate with a few drops of water. Line the pie plate with two 12-inch pieces of plastic wrap, allowing the wrap to hang over the sides of the dish. (The plastic lining will make it easier to get the pie out of the pan when it is ready to serve.) To prepare the pecans, combine the water and sugar in a small saucepan and bring to a boil. Add the curry, butter, and salt and stir until the butter has melted. Place the pecans in a bowl and pour the warm syrup over them, tossing to coat well. Spread the pecans in a single layer on a baking sheet using an offset spatula. Bake for 25 minutes, stirring every 5 minutes, until the nuts are nicely roasted. Let the pecans cool.

Meanwhile, place the milk chocolate in a microwave-safe bowl and microwave on high, at 30-second intervals, stirring in between, until melted. Once the pecans have cooled, choose about ¾ cup of the nicest-looking nuts to use as garnish and set them aside.

Place the remaining pecans in a food processor and pulse until coarsely ground. Stir the ground pecans into the melted chocolate and pour into the plastic-lined pie dish. Cover the mixture with another piece of plastic wrap and press it into the bottom and sides of the pie dish to form an even crust. Place the dish in the freezer for 15 minutes.

To prepare the filling, combine all the ingredients in a microwave-safe bowl. Microwave on high for 1 minute, then whisk vigorously. Repeat this process four more times, until the mixture comes to a boil and thickens.

Using the overhanging plastic film, lift the crust from the pie pan, peel off the plastic wrap, and return the crust to the pan. Pour the cooled filling mixture into the piecrust and let it sit for 10 minutes. Arrange the reserved nuts decoratively on top and refrigerate the pie for about 1 hour, or until firm.

Whip the cream in the bowl of a stand mixer fitted with the whisk attachment, adding the sugar little by little until firm. Transfer it to a clean bowl and refrigerate until ready to serve.

Cut the pie into slices and serve with a dollop of whipped cream.

Note: You can get sorghum molasses online at http://www.newsomscountry ham.com/sormol.html

Pineapple Coconut Upside-Down Cake

I liked this cake even before I tasted it. The idea of a cake being upside down appeals to the spirit of fun that defines dessert. That spirit—being willing to look at things from a new perspective—is something I have always admired about this country. Maybe that's why America has so many inventors. I've been told that the classic recipe for this cake appeared in a number of places shortly after the Dole Food Company began to export mass quantities of pineapple in the 1920s. Here, instead of the traditional yellow cake, I added shredded coconut to my sponge cake. Why? Well, if I think about Hawaii and picture a pineapple plantation, I think of coconut palm trees swaying in the breeze. And then I think about the beach, and maybe a long, cold daiquiri, which leads me to a powerfully sweet sauce, laced with rum. ✳ SERVES 8

PINEAPPLE TOPPING AND RUM SAUCE

1 cup water

1½ cups packed brown sugar, dark
   or light

1 large pineapple, trimmed, cored,
   and cut into ½-inch pieces,
   trimmings saved

4 tablespoons (½ stick) unsalted butter

⅓ cup rum

CAKE

¼ cup unsweetened shredded
   dried coconut

¼ cup powdered sugar

4 eggs

⅓ cup granulated sugar

¼ cup Wondra flour

Start the pineapple topping by bringing the water and 1 cup of the brown sugar to a boil in a medium saucepan. Add 3 cups of the diced pineapple and simmer for 5 minutes. Using a colander, strainer, or slotted spoon, remove the pineapple, leaving the cooking liquid in the pan. Place the cooked fruit on a plate lined with paper towels to absorb the excess liquid. Cool to room temperature.

Begin the rum sauce by adding all the remaining uncooked fruit pieces, including the pineapple trimmings, to the reserved pan of liquid. Simmer for 30 minutes, uncovered, then let the sauce cool until just warm to the touch. Transfer it to a blender and puree until smooth. Pour it through a fine-mesh strainer. Stir in the rum and set aside.

Prepare the cake pan: Using a pencil, trace around the bottom of a 9-inch cake pan onto a piece of parchment. Cut out the round, making it slightly smaller than the circle so it will fit perfectly. Lightly coat the inside of the pan with cooking spray and press the parchment circle inside.

Finish the pineapple topping by placing the remaining brown sugar and the butter into a medium saucepan. Bring the mixture to a slow boil and simmer gently for 3 minutes. Remove the pan from the heat and add the cooled, diced pineapple, mixing with a rubber spatula so that each piece is well coated. Pour the caramelized pineapple into the prepared cake pan.

Preheat the oven to 325 degrees.

To make the cake batter, pulse the coconut and powdered sugar in a blender or food processor until finely ground. Place the eggs in the bowl of a stand mixer fitted with the whisk attachment and beat on high for about 1 minute, until the eggs are foamy. Add the granulated sugar 1 tablespoon at a time and continue whipping for 10 minutes on high (you can't overwhip this). Switching to a rubber spatula, gently fold in the flour and the coconut sugar mixture. Mix until the flour is just incorporated. Pour the batter over the topping in the cake pan and bake for 40 minutes. Let the cake cool for 30 minutes.

To unmold the pineapple cake, run a thin knife blade around the inside of the pan. Next, set your serving plate upside down on top of the cake mold and flip pan and plate together. Remove and discard the parchment paper circle. Cut the cake and serve it with pineapple rum sauce poured over each slice.

Fourth of July Tart

With caramelized marshmallow, silky whipped cream, crisp meringue, and a bunch of berries, this tart has all the colors of the Fourth of July, and it's as much fun as summer. If you asked a child to dream up a perfect dessert, I think it would look like this. We didn't have marshmallows in France when I was young, so I think of this cake as a true marriage of French and American desserts: marshmallows and meringue. My marshmallow recipe is super fast to make and plenty sweet, yet it has much less sugar than many homemade marshmallow recipes. There is more than enough sweetness in the other components—the marshmallow doesn't need to be so sugary that it makes your teeth chatter. Also I cut down on the amount of water. Remember there is a lot of water in the egg whites. The result is less rubbery, somewhere between a marshmallow and a mousse. Maybe it should be called a "moussemallow."

Note: For easy assembly, make the meringue and the marshmallow the day before. If you have extra meringue, pipe it into any shape you like and bake.

* SERVES 6 TO 8

4 egg whites

1 pinch salt

½ cup sugar

4 teaspoons unflavored gelatin

2 tablespoons cold water

4 egg whites

¾ cup sugar

2 ounces white chocolate

1 cup strawberries, washed and
trimmed

1 cup raspberries, washed

1 cup blueberries, washed, stems
removed

1 cup heavy cream

2 tablespoons sugar

Red Berry Coulis (page 53)

Vanilla ice cream for serving
(optional)

Preheat the oven to 220 degrees.

Place the egg whites and salt in the bowl of a stand mixer fitted with the whisk attachment and beat on high for about 1 minute, until the whites are foamy. Add the sugar 1 tablespoon at a time and continue beating until stiff peaks are formed, about 7 minutes. Line a sheet pan with parchment paper. Using a 9-inch plate, draw a circle on the parchment paper, flip the paper over, and place it in the center of the sheet pan. Attach a ¾-inch tip to a pastry bag and fill it with the meringue. Starting in the center of the circle, pipe the meringue in a clockwise spiral pattern until you reach the outer edge of the circle. This will be the base of the tart. To create the edge of the tart, pipe small dollops of meringue around the perimeter, giving the effect of a crown. Bake the meringue for 2 hours, then turn off the oven and leave the meringue inside until about 1 hour before you want to serve the dessert.

Make the marshmallow by whisking the gelatin and water together in a microwave-safe bowl until well blended. Microwave for 30 seconds to ensure that the gelatin is melted and hot. Whisk again and set the bowl aside. Place the egg whites in the bowl of a stand mixer fitted with the whisk attachment and beat on high for about 1 minute, until the whites are foamy. Add the sugar 1 tablespoon at a time until soft peaks are formed, 3 or 4 minutes. Stop the mixer and add the melted gelatin to the bowl, then whip on high again for a few seconds. Lightly coat a 9-inch square pan with cooking spray and line it with plastic wrap. Spread the marshmallow into the pan and cover it with another piece of plastic wrap. Smooth and flatten the marshmallow with your hands and refrigerate for 30 minutes.

(The meringue and marshmallows can be made to this point a day ahead of time.)

Once the meringue shell is at room temperature, microwave the white chocolate on high at 30-second intervals, stirring in between, until it is melted. This shouldn't take much longer than a minute. With a pastry brush, brush the melted chocolate over the inside surface of the meringue shell. This creates a moisture barrier and keeps the meringue crunchy. Place the meringue shell in the refrigerator for about 10 minutes, but no longer, to set the chocolate.

Cut the strawberries into bite-size pieces if they are large. Place them along with the raspberries and blueberries into a medium bowl and set aside. Whip the cream in the chilled bowl of a stand mixer fitted with the whisk attachment, adding the sugar little by little until firm.

Preheat the broiler.

Spread the whipped cream into the bottom of the meringue shell. Pour the fruit on top. Remove the marshmallow from the pan with the help of the plastic wrap and place on a clean work surface and cut it into 1-inch squares. Arrange the marshmallows liberally on top of the fruit. Broil the tart for 1 minute, until the marshmallows are lightly toasted. Alternatively, if you have a small blowtorch, use it to brown the marshmallows.

To serve, cut large slices and spoon red berry coulis on top. For an extra-rich dessert, serve it with ice cream.

Lightened-Up Cheesecake with Cocoa Cranberry Topping

When I first heard of it, the idea of cheesecake seemed strange. What could it possibly mean? A Camembert cake? You might just as well have suggested a roast beef cookie. We didn't make cakes from cheese in France.

I soon realized that we had overlooked a wonderful dessert. I also found that a little goes a long way: the classic American recipe is very heavy. Basically, it's flan plus cream cheese plus a lot of sugar. This variation is much lighter—more of a soufflé than a flan—and though it is called cake, it requires no baking. This means that it involves less work, and also that there is no possibility of the kind of cracking that often blemishes regular cheesecakes. For the filling, I omit the egg yolk from the classic recipe and substitute gelatin and whipped cream. The crust is a little bit of France and a whole lot of America. The cornflakes are pure crunch. They are close in texture and lightness of taste to a standard French baker's product called *feuillantine*, which is nothing more than crunchy bits of leftover crepe batter. I hit upon the technique of combining the cornflakes with chocolate and peanut butter in a microwave; and later, guests and journalists compared the result to a Kit Kat bar. The oil from the nuts makes the chocolate more tender, while the chocolate coating keeps the cornflake bits nice and crunchy.

* SERVES 8

CRUST

3 ounces semisweet chocolate,
    coarsely chopped, or
    ½ cup semisweet chocolate chips
2 tablespoons creamy peanut butter

2 cups cornflakes, roughly crushed
  with the hands

FILLING

1½ teaspoons unflavored gelatin

Juice of 1 lemon (2 tablespoons)

1 cup heavy cream

8 ounces (1 package) cream cheese,
  at room temperature

2 egg whites

½ cup granulated sugar

CHOCOLATE TOPPING

½ cup cranberry juice

2 tablespoons alkalized
  (Dutch process) cocoa powder

1 teaspoon unflavored gelatin

Start by making the crust. In a microwave-safe bowl, micro-wave the chocolate on high at 30-second intervals, stirring in between, until melted. Add the peanut butter and mix with a whisk until well blended. Add the cornflakes and gently stir with a rubber spatula to coat them. Line a sheet pan with a piece of plastic wrap. Place a bottomless 8-inch cake ring or an 8-by-2-inch springform pan with the bottom removed on top of the plastic wrap and pour the chocolaty cornflakes into the ring. Laying a second piece of plastic wrap on top, use your fingers to push the mixture flat into the bottom. Leave the plastic in place and put the crust in the freezer for 10 minutes to set.

Make the filling by mixing the gelatin, lemon juice, and 3 tablespoons of the heavy cream in a microwave-safe bowl. Whisk to blend well and microwave for 1 minute. Stir, cover, and set aside.

Place the cream cheese in the bowl of a stand mixer fixed with the paddle attachment and whip on high for 1 minute or until soft. Transfer the cream cheese to a medium bowl. Wash and dry the mixer bowl and whisk. Pour the remaining heavy cream into the clean mixer bowl and whip it on high to form soft peaks. Spoon the whipped cream onto the cream cheese mixture, but do not mix.

Wash and dry the mixer bowl and whisk again. Place the egg whites in the bowl of the stand mixer fitted with the whisk attachment and beat on high for about 1 minute, until the whites are foamy. Add the sugar 1 tablespoon at a time. Once the sugar is all in, continue whipping for about 3 minutes. Add the gelatin mixture to the bowl with the cream cheese and whipped cream and blend with a whisk. Gently fold in the whipped egg whites with a large rubber spatula as quickly as possible.

Place your serving dish next to the ring containing the frozen cornflake crust and gently lift the plastic to remove the crust and place it on the serving dish. Discard the plastic. Replace the cake ring around the crust on the serving plate. Pour the filling over the crust, spreading it to the edges of the pan and smoothing it with an offset spatula. Freeze the cake for at least 1 hour.

Meanwhile in a small saucepan, whisk the ingredients for the chocolate topping together. Over medium heat, warm the liquid to just melt the gelatin, then let the liquid cool to body temperature. Pour the cooled topping over the cheesecake and replace it in the freezer for at least 30 minutes—this is the minimum amount of time it will take the topping to set, but you can store the cake in the freezer for up to 1 month.

About 4 hours before serving, wet a dish towel with hot water, squeeze out the excess water, and place it around the sides of the pan. The metal will heat up and make the ring easier to remove. Lift the ring, set it aside, and place the cake in the refrigerator to thaw completely before serving.

Cherry Chocolate Layer Cake

If you have ever made a Black Forest cake or Sacher torte, you will find that this cake is no less pleasing but much easier. It is also as good a place as any for me to come clean with a confession that has been weighing on my soul for more than thirty years.

One day I was on a catering delivery for a wedding. I was running late with the cake. It was very hot outside, and my delivery van was not air-conditioned in the back. As I took a turn on the roads of LA, the cake box smashed into the side of the cargo space and one of the two turtledoves on top of the cake decided to fly away! Upon arriving at the party, I brought the cake to the refrigerator and attempted to make it fit, but it was a very big and heavy cake, and as I let go of it, the shelf in the refrigerator decided to break! Now the cake was missing two turtledoves and had a rather crunched appearance. Then, to make matters worse, the fridge door wouldn't close! The cake was too big! So I propped a box against it to hold it closed and I ran to the kitchen to see how the rest of the food was going. When I returned to see the cake—which I had every intention of repairing—I found a great excuse in the form of the owner's two big Labradors. They were madly sniffing around the refrigerator door, so I opened it for them, nudging their muzzles into my cake. At that point, I shouted for the owner to come quickly and see the tragedy that had befallen her cake. She apologized profusely about her dogs, led them away, and begged me to do what I could to fix the cake.

"Madame," I said with a courtly bow, "I will do everything within my powers to repair your cake." Which I did with a few fresh strawberries and some whipped cream. It wasn't exactly what she or I had imagined, but the guests never knew the difference.

I'm glad I had this chance to come clean with my conscience. Thank you, dear readers. * SERVES 8

FLOURLESS CHOCOLATE LAYER CAKE

9 ounces semisweet chocolate

5 eggs, separated

½ cup sugar

1 recipe Cocoa Puff Chocolate
  Mousse Cups (page 32)

TOPPINGS

1 cup water

½ cup plus 2 tablespoons sugar

1½ pounds cherries, stemmed and
  pitted ¼ cup kirsch

1 cup heavy cream

8 ounces dark chocolate for shaving

Preheat the oven to 325 degrees. Cut a piece of parchment to fit the bottom of a 9-by-13-inch pan. Using cooking spray, lightly coat the inside of the sheet pan and place the parchment in it.

In a medium microwave-safe bowl, microwave the chocolate on high at 30-second intervals, stirring in between, until melted.

Meanwhile, in a stand mixer fitted with the whisk attachment, beat the egg yolks with ¼ cup of the sugar on high for 5 minutes. Pour the egg yolk mixture on top of the room-temperature melted chocolate, but do not mix it yet.

Wash and dry the stand mixer bowl and whisk. Place the egg whites in the bowl of the stand mixer fitted with the whisk attachment and beat on high for about 1 minute, until the whites are foamy. Add the remaining sugar 1 tablespoon at a time, then reduce the mixer speed to low until soft peaks form, about 5 minutes total mixing time.

While the egg whites are whisking, use a rubber spatula to combine the chocolate and egg yolks. When the whites are ready, gently incorporate them into the chocolate mixture as well.

Pour the batter into the prepared pan and spread it out evenly with an offset spatula until it reaches the sides. Bake for 35 minutes, or until it is set and a toothpick or knife inserted in the center comes out clean. Cool the cake completely in the pan.

Cut the cooled cake in half crosswise so that you have two pieces, each 6½ by 9 inches. Place a cake half on a serving plate. Spoon the chocolate mousse on top and spread it evenly over the surface with an offset spatula. Gently press the second cake half onto the mousse. Refrigerate for 1 hour.

Meanwhile, make the cherry topping by bringing the water and ½ cup of the sugar to a boil in a small saucepan. Add the cherries, reduce the heat, and simmer for 5 minutes. Remove the pan from the heat and let the cherries cool in the syrup. Strain the cooled cherries, saving the syrup. Place the syrup, kirsch, and ½ cup cherries in a blender. Puree on high until smooth.

Whip the cream in the chilled bowl of a stand mixer fitted with the whisk attachment, adding the remaining 2 tablespoons sugar little by little until firm. Transfer to a clean bowl and refrigerate.

Before serving, cut the cake into 8 equal pieces. Place each one on a dessert plate and let rest at room temperature for 1 hour. To serve, top each slice with a few cherries and a dollop of whipped cream. Drizzle cherry sauce around the slice and, using a vegetable peeler, shave some chocolate on top of the whole piece.

A Happy Birthday Cake

There is no rule that says you have to serve this as a birthday cake, but I have done so many times because it has such a fun look—light as a smile. The inspiration is a traditional French cake called a *fraisier*, but while preserving its delightful appearance, I use much less egg yolk and sugar. My family is not a big fan of buttercream, but they always dig into this lighter version with passion. Whipping makes it airy and mousse-like. Finally, whipped cream on top, instead of the traditional marzipan, has the same airy effect. The soaking syrup of orange juice and sugar replaces the French combination of kirsch and simple syrup, and I say good riddance! Whenever you can add flavor, reduce alcohol, and avoid simple syrup . . . please do so.

Note: I call for one less egg in this sponge cake than in my standard genoise. It is lighter.

Remember to take this from the fridge two hours before serving; otherwise, you will think you are eating a stick of butter. ✳ SERVES 8

CAKE
3 eggs, separated
½ cup sugar
¾ cup all-purpose flour, sifted

SOAKING SYRUP
1 cup orange juice
½ cup sugar

BUTTERCREAM AND STRAWBERRY FILLINGS
¼ cup plus 2 tablespoons sugar
1 teaspoon vanilla extract
2 egg yolks
2 tablespoons cornstarch

✳

CARAMEL SAUCE

This bittersweet sauce can be used on ice cream, over apple desserts, or as a dip for apple wedges, and is delicious eaten all by itself. The darker the sugar gets, the less sweet the sauce will be. Cook it to a golden brown color if you want the maximum sweetness or to a deep mahogany brown if you would like it more bittersweet. Test a small spoonful on a white plate or bowl to gauge the color more accurately.

1½ cups sugar
About ¾ cup water
1¼ cups heavy cream, plus more for serving, if needed

Place the sugar in a heavy medium saucepan. Add the water gradually—you want to add just enough to bring the (continued)

✳

*

sugar to the consistency of wet sand. Cook over low heat until the sugar dissolves, swirling the pan occasionally but not stirring. Increase the heat to medium and boil, still without stirring, until the sugar caramelizes and turns a deep brown, 7 to 10 minutes. Watch carefully so the mixture doesn't burn. Remove the hot pan from the heat, place a strainer over the saucepan, and gradually and carefully pour in the cream. (The strainer prevents dangerous splattering from the hot caramel.) Carefully stir in the cream, return the pan to low heat, and simmer the sauce, stirring occasionally, until it is smooth and thick, about 3 minutes. Cool, cover, and refrigerate. This caramel

(continued)

*

1 cup milk
1 cup (2 sticks) unsalted butter,
   softened
2 quarts strawberries, washed

WHIPPED CREAM
1 cup heavy cream
2 tablespoons sugar

Preheat the oven to 350 degrees.

Place the egg whites in the bowl of a stand mixer fitted with the whisk attachment and whisk on high for about 1 minute, until the whites are foamy. Add the sugar 1 tablespoon at a time until stiff peaks have formed, 5 to 7 minutes. Stir the egg yolks together in a small bowl. Add the egg yolks and the flour to the beaten egg whites and whisk on low speed for a few seconds. Remove the bowl from the mixer and finish incorporating the ingredients with a rubber spatula until well blended.

Place an 8-by-2½-inch cake ring or a springform pan without the bottom on a sheet pan lined with Silpat or parchment. Pour the batter into the ring and bake for 25 minutes, until the cake is lightly brown or a cake tester inserted in the center comes out clean. Cool the cake in the pan for at least 1 hour or up to overnight. (This cake can be done a day before, or you can use a frozen, defrosted cake that you have baked in advance.)

Meanwhile, make the soaking syrup by bringing the orange juice and sugar to a boil in a medium saucepan. Cook the syrup for 1 minute, then remove it from the heat and let cool.

Start the cream filling by whisking ¼ cup of the sugar with the vanilla, egg yolks, cornstarch, and milk in a small microwave-safe bowl. Cook for 3 minutes on high, whisking vigorously halfway through and again at the end of cooking. Cover the bowl with plastic wrap, placing the wrap directly on the surface of the filling to prevent a skin from forming, and refrigerate for at least 1 hour.

Choose 8 large strawberries that are about the same shape and cut them in half. Place the cut sides down and trim them at the stem end so that the strawberries are all uniform in size. Cut a ¼-inch slice from the flat inside surface of each of the strawberry halves and set the slices aside for decoration. Reserve the remaining strawberry pieces separately.

Run the blade of a thin knife around the inside of the cake ring to separate it from the cake or open the latch of the springform pan. Using a serrated knife, carefully slice the cake horizontally into equal layers. Set aside.

Wash and dry the cake ring. Cut two pieces of parchment and place them under the cake ring on a serving plate, letting them overlap in the center of the ring. (This helps you keep the plate clean.) Place the top piece of cake into the ring, cut side up. Spoon half of the soaking liquid onto the cake. Press the strawberry slices, standing upright with the points at the top, around the inside of the cake ring.

Trim and chop the remaining whole strawberries and the reserved berry pieces and place them in a bowl with the remaining 2 tablespoons sugar. Stir to coat and set aside.

To finish the buttercream, whisk the cooled pastry cream vigorously by hand, or in a stand mixer fitted with a whisk attachment. Cut up the softened butter, add it to the bowl, and whisk again until it's all incorporated and has the consistency of mayonnaise.

*

will keep for several days in the refrigerator. To serve, warm it over medium heat until melted and thin it with additional cream or milk if needed.

*

Spoon half of the buttercream into the prepared cake ring. Spread all the chopped strawberries on top and press them into the cream. Reserve 2 tablespoons buttercream in a small bowl and add the rest on top of the strawberries, smoothing the surface evenly. The filling should reach the tops of the strawberry slices inside the cake ring. Place the second slice of cake on top of the cream, cut side up, fitting the layer inside the ring of strawberries but not covering the decorative ones on the outside, and soak it with the remaining orange syrup. Spread the reserved 2 tablespoons buttercream on top of the cake. Refrigerate for about 4 hours or overnight.

Before serving, whip the cream in the chilled bowl of a stand mixer fitted with the whisk attachment, adding the sugar little by little until firm. Spoon it on top of the cake and flatten it out to the edges of the cake ring. Remove the parchment paper by pulling the pieces out from under the cake. Hold a warm, damp towel around the cake ring for a few seconds. This will allow the cake ring to separate from the cake more easily. Remove the ring and voilà! You have a beautiful birthday cake!

Notes from the Test Kitchen: Mondays with Michel

If you walk into the kitchen of Citronelle on almost any given day you will find Michel sitting at the large wooden chef's table, rubbing his beard, poring over a recipe, scribbling down notes. This table is the heart of the restaurant, where Michel holds court. Each person who works in the kitchen comes to the table first to greet him and shake his hand—"Hello, Chef," "Good morning, Chef"—and then it's off to work. Sometimes former employees, fellow chefs, or family members stop by. If Michel is not at the table you might find him scurrying around the kitchen—stirring, whisking, pouring, tasting. A culinary Saint Nicholas; an artist in the process of creation.

It has been our privilege to work with this inspiring chef on this project. A morning in his kitchen is always an adventure, when hours go by full of "what if" experimentation, and hard work feels suspiciously like play. When we first started working with Michel Richard, one of our colleagues, a pastry chef who had worked with him previously, described his process by gesturing toward a cake of fresh yeast sitting on the marble counter and saying, "Michel Richard is the kind of chef who might look at that yeast and wonder, 'What else can we do with this besides leaven dough? Fry it. See what happens.'" Then he continued, "If you are open to being creative in the kitchen, you'll be fine. But if you can't get past a traditional way of doing things, you'll die there."

While Michel is constantly looking for interesting ways to make food more delicious, it is always with his audience in mind. He lavishes attention on everything he makes, approaching each recipe with respect and love for both the diner and the baker. One day, on a break from testing recipes in the kitchen at Citronelle—a morning when only one of the things we made really "worked"—we walked over to a nearby restaurant for a late lunch. When our appetizers came, Michel took one bite and exclaimed playfully yet passionately, "Where is the love in this dish? Why does the chef hate me?" After a few more bites, he put down his fork and declared, with a twinkle in his eye, "Whoever made this should be taken in the back and shot." For him there is no excuse for not making your guests happy.

This attention to his audience shines through in his ingredient choices. While Michel is an incredibly accomplished chef, with every ingredient available to him, he is never a snob about food. He will use any ingredient he thinks will make his food better: Cream of Wheat, Cocoa Puffs, Rice Krispies, bacon. He plays with corn flour, rice flour, potato flour, almond flour. He is constantly looking for methods that will make things simpler for people to make seemingly intimidating, beautiful desserts. Who can't make pastry cream and lemon curd in the microwave? Why not temper chocolate in the microwave, too?

The strength of this book is that while Michel is permanently rooted in rigorous, classical French baking methods, he demystifies the "magic" behind desserts that look complicated. In *Sweet Magic* he does for French pastry what Julia Child did for cuisine, showing that really anyone can make puff pastry or éclairs at home. He consistently talks about how to make things simpler, less expensive, and more accessible to his readers. These recipes are a result of this focus and center on taking a few high-quality ingredients, combining them in a streamlined but proven method, and coming up with something both beautiful and delicious.

The notes and the essays in this book both empower and challenge the home chef. Michel gives alternatives for special commercial pans, equipment, and ingredients. The results are a show-stopping dessert or something quick and homey. In *Sweet Magic*, Michel Richard simplifies professional chef techniques, pulling back the curtain from the magic of dessert, and showing the easiest ways to get there. You can trust him to show you the best, most delicious way to make your dessert. Our hope is that when you try these recipes you will have as much fun making and eating them as we did.

Wendy Ripley and Jack Revelle
Washington, D.C.

Acknowledgments

If I thanked everybody, I would need two books. Here are the people who made this book possible. My executive chef at Citronelle, David Deshaies, who cheerfully "allowed" me to use my restaurant's kitchen to test my recipes. Also: his colleague and executive sous chef, Thomas Hauck, who selflessly put on 20 pounds in the tasting—I mean testing—process; Mark Courseille, pastry chef at Citronelle, who knows my recipes better than anyone else (sometimes better than me); the indefatigable Wendy Ripley and Jack Revelle, for testing and writing these recipes for the home *patissier* or *patissière*. Oops, don't let me forget Miss Nora Ripley-Grant, who personally oversaw the testing of the Maple Pudding and Charlotte Nora; the eagle eye and delicate pen of Marion Rosenfeld, who reviewed and massaged every word; her valiant husband, Thomas Jones, pastry chef instructor at the French

Culinary Institute, who cast his professorial eye on the recipes; Libby Edelson at Ecco, for her tireless attention to detail; Dan Halpern, for believing in us and for putting up with my sangfroid; Lisa Queen, the best agent in the entire world; my buddy Peter Kaminsky; my "brain" and my assistant Mel Davis; and my unbelievably lovely wife, Laurence, who was there at the conception of every recipe, testing it for the first time, writing it, and most of all, for being my soul mate.

P.S. I would also like to thank the medieval monk who perfected *côte rôti*e. I would probably go to church more if they used it for the sacrament.

Index

Filling (*Bavaroise*), 95, 97
  whipped, making, 39, 40
Cream Puff Batter (*Pâte à Chou*), Quicker,
    104–5
  Chocolate Éclairs, 100–103
  Chocolate Saint-Honoré Lulu,
    106–8
  Strawberry Cream Puffs with a
    Caramel Halo, 170–71
Crème Anglaise, Cinnamon (Cinnamon
    Custard Sauce), 163–64
crème brûlée
  Coffee, 26–28
  Sandwich, 109–11
Crepes, Rum Apple, 88–91
crunch helpers, 136–37
crusts
  Chocolate, Peanut Butter, and
    Cornflake, 182–83
  see also pie crusts
curry
  Corn Cookies with a Smidgen of,
    148–49
  Cranberry Cream, Quick Pecan Pie
    with Sorghum Molasses and,
    172–74
custard(s), 18
  Cinnamon Crème Anglaise (Cinnamon
    Custard Sauce), 163–64
  Coffee Crème Brûlée, 26–28
  Flan with Automatic Crust, 35–36
  Maple Pudding with Strawberry Coulis
    and Lemon Milk Foam, 157–59
  nickname for, 157
  Strawberry Milk, Raspberry Tartlet
    with, 47–49
  Ultimate French Toast, 23–25

doggie bags, 137
Doughnuts, Baked, 152–53
doughs, 14–15
  Almond Sugar (*Pâte Sucrée*), 146–47
  Brioche, 81–82
  Cocoa Sugar (*Pâte Sucrée*), 169
  Linzer, 45–46
  Puff Pastry, 50–52

éclairs, 14–15
  Chocolate, 100–103
egg(s), 6–7, 10, 14, 77
  Flan with Automatic Crust, 35–36
  Ultimate French Toast, 23–25
  whites. *See* meringue(s)
Espresso Rum Mousse, 39–40
ethnic markets, 35
Extremely Chocolaty Chip Cookies,
    142–44

fennel, 11
feuillantine, 182
fig(s)
  Apple Crumple, 160–62
  pectin in, 12
fillings
  Buttercream, 189–91
  Chocolate Whipped Cream,
    113, 114
  Cream (*Bavaroise*), 95, 97
  Marshmallow Buttercream, 59–60
flan
  with Automatic Crust, 35–36
  Crème Brûlée Sandwich, 109–11
  Ultimate French Toast, 23–25

Vacherin, 126–28
vanilla bean(s)
   Flan with Automatic Crust, 35–36
   seeds, avoiding lumps of, when adding
      them to a liquid, 27n
   Ultimate French Toast, 23–25

whipped cream
   Chocolate, Filling, 113, 114
   making, 39, 40

white chocolate, in Fourth of July Tart,
   178–81
World's Flakiest Apple Pie, 163–65
World's Flakiest Cherry Pie, 166–67

xantham gum, 37